Concerning

the

Disciples of Christ

A Restoration Movement Workbook

BY

B. B. TYLER,

Author of the *History of the Disciples of Christ* in the American Church History Series

INTRODUCTION BY

F. D. POWER

Author of *Sketches of Our Pioneers: A Brief Restoration Movement History*

EDITED AND ANOTATED BY

BRADLEY S. COBB

Editor of *Alexander Campbell: A Collection (two volumes),* etc.

Cobb Publishing
www.TheCobbSix.com

2016

Published in the United States by Cobb Publishing
(www.TheCobbSix.com)

Contact Cobb Publishing:
Phone: (405) 964-3082
Email: Admin@TheCobbSix.com
Mail: Cobb Publishing, 827 Steed, McLoud, OK 74851

ISBN:
978-0692610923
ISBN-10: 0692610928

CONTENTS

CONTENTS

FOREWORD

This short work on the Restoration Movement has undergone several changes from its original printing. We have taken the liberty of making several corrections (typos, grammar, etc)., as well as updating some of the language (removing the dreaded –eth words) to make it easier for modern readers to understand.

In addition to these changes, we have also added several footnotes to explain certain words and phrases, as well as making any observations we feel are needed or useful throughout the text.

B.B. Tyler originally penned these words in 1897, less than a decade before the U.S. Census formally recognized a division between the "Christian Church" (also called "Disciples of Christ") and the "church of Christ." The missionary society, one of the main points of disagreement between the two sides, is boasted about in a later chapter, with no discussion of the division it helped cause.

We have taken the time to prepare this book for publication because we believe that it is a good, valuable overview of the Restoration Movement and the cause for which we plead. We hope you find this updated version of *Concerning the Disciples of Christ* to be worthwhile.

Bradley Cobb
2016

INTRODUCTION

No chapter in American church history—none, we may truly say, in universal church history—is more fascinating than that of the work inaugurated by the Campbells and their co-laborers.[1] No religious movement of the century has been more important and wide-reaching in its purpose; none has had in its early struggles and progress more of the heroic element; none has been more effective if we view its results. Its origin, genius and growth are more and more attracting the attention and even the wonder of thoughtful people. This study must be useful to everyone who would be properly informed on the live issues of the day, and eminently so to the hundreds of thousands of young men and women who now constitute this marvelously growing body of believers. To one who has all his life been associated with this religious movement, and whose service has been conspicuously faithful and successful, was assigned the work of preparing these pages. The task has been well-performed.

It will be noted that this claims simply to be a hand-book. It contains the seeds of things. It couldn't be expected that the writer would

---

[1] Mr. Power, author of *Sketches of Our Pioneers*, neglects to take into consideration that the attempts at Restoration were already in full-swing before Campbell ever came to America. Chapter two of this very work discusses some of those who went before him. At the same time, it is understandable that some of the men of Mr. Power's time sought to distance themselves from men like Abner Jones, James O'Kelly, and others who became known as the *Christian Connexion*, because preachers from the *Connexion* (such as Nicholas Summerbell and Matthew Gardner) had begun to actively oppose the Disciples of Christ in books, tracts, periodicals, and pulpits.

choose a wider scope or give more elaborate details than will be found in this small volume. It is intended to be a guide to the reader, a manual setting forth in brief outline the matters with which it deals, and leaving the student to take up any line of thought suggested by its chapters and indulge in the largest liberty of investigation.

Very profitably and judiciously the author discusses his subject under twenty-two divisions. In the use of this volume by the individual reader or by the circle there is suggestion here of wide fields of research. In connection with the first five chapters very profitable study can be made of the Renaissance and the Lutheran Reformation, and of the great characters to whom the world is specially indebted for its escape from the dark ages and its advance to the present high state of civilization and religious liberty. In the development of the line of thought from chapters six to twelve a series of studies of the Acts of the Apostles, of the cases of conversion reported there, of apostolic church organization and church life could be pursued to great advantage.

In taking up chapters thirteen to twenty-two, which deal with present conditions among the Disciples, the whole field of modern religious thought and action, literature, education, missionary effort, charity and temperance work, is opened before us. Throughout the course of study such books as the lives of Alexander Campbell, Scott, Smith, Errett, and others should be read, sketches of these leaders prepared and read before the circles, and their works reviewed.[1]

We commend this little work and this line of collateral study to young and old as of profound interest, of untold value, and of present pressing need.

F. D. Power.
Washington, D. C.

---

[1] Mr. Power himself prepared many such sketches, which are compiled in the book, *Sketches of Our Pioneers: A Brief Restoration Movement History*

Chapter One

RELIGIOUS CONDITIONS

As we begin the study of the people known as the disciples of Christ,[1] let us spend a few moments in looking at the moral and spiritual condition of the people of the United States in the early part of the nineteenth century.

A picture of this period, fully and accurately drawn, would be dark in the extreme. It was a time of prevalent unbelief. The uneducated and the cultured were both, to an alarming extent, under the dark pall[2] of infidelity. It was thought by some that the Christian religion was destined to pass away, and soon. A better system, it was thought, would take its place. Religion was blamed for most of the evils from which men suffered. If every religion could be removed, man would at once enter into such prosperity, in almost every respect, as he had never before experienced.

---

[1] This term, *disciples of Christ* was the one preferred by Alexander Campbell, though it was used interchangeably with "church of Christ" and "Christian Church" during the 1800s. By the beginning of the 1900s, most—if not all—of the congregations who rejected the addition of instrumental music had stopped using the designation "*disciples*" when describing themselves. They have almost universally chosen to be known as "churches of Christ."

[2] A *pall* is a dark covering, oftentimes referring to a thick, black sheet that covers a coffin. Other times, the word refers to dark clouds hovering overhead. Either way, it's not a good thing.

Among those who believed in God, in Jesus, and in the Bible, the prevalent thought was Calvinistic. They held that a definite number of men were foreordained to everlasting life, regardless of belief or conduct. Those who were not thus elected to life in Christ, were children of wrath. It was thought that there is nothing for a man to do in order to secure salvation. Every case of regeneration was as much a miracle as the restoration of Lazarus to life. Pious men objected to the minister speaking to their sons and daughters on the subject of personal religion. They said: "If they are the elect of God, he will regenerate them in His own time, and in His own way. To talk to them, urging them to become Christians, may make them hypocrites." The Rev. Dr. Dorchester, in his book entitled "Christianity in the United States," says that "the most pious people in the United States in the beginning of the present century entertained a faith so different from the present belief of evangelical Christians as to almost create the impression, on our minds, that *their* religion was not the same religion which *we* now have, and in which *we* believe."

The word of God, given in the Bible, was regarded as a dead letter. There was no power in the Gospel to produce faith. The faith by which men are saved, it was understood, was a direct gift from God. Faith didn't come as a result of hearing God's testimony. The Sunday school met with serious opposition. Bible and tract societies were supposed to exist contrary to the will of God. The names of congregations cooperating in mission and Sunday school work, and in the distribution of the Word of God through the agency of Bible societies, were, at least by one association of Baptist churches, removed from its minutes— they would not recognize them as their brethren. Persons who engaged in such enterprises were condemned as heretics!

The moral life of the people was on a very low plane. Human slavery existed without rebuke.[1] Men and women were bought and sold at

---

[1] This statement, while perhaps generally true of most people, is not completely accurate. There were several prominent people who opposed slavery in the last 1700s in the United States. But slavery was still allowed by law throughout the country.

public auction, like cattle and mules. Difficulties between "gentlemen" were settled by fighting duels. Reputable "gentlemen" drank to intoxication. There was no total abstinence sentiment in those days. Alcoholic drink was believed to be a good creature of God. Members of churches drank until they were drunk.

Even supposed ministers of the Gospel sometimes indulged to excess in the use of alcoholic liquors. The Lord's Day was habitually desecrated.

Imagine the condition society would be in, at the present time, if Sunday Schools, Bible and missionary societies, Societies of Christian Endeavor, temperance societies, etc., etc., were blotted out. In the days now under review there were no union meetings. The prevalent sectarian spirit rendered such evangelistic efforts in behalf of lost men impossible. The churches, instead of cooperating in efforts to spread abroad among men the light of the Gospel of the Prince of Peace, were engaged in fighting against each other.

What were some of the causes producing this sad condition of faith and life?

Before the War of Independence, Great Britain would not permit the publication of the Bible within the limits of her dependencies on this side of the Atlantic. There came to be, therefore, a famine of the Word of God.

The aid rendered by France to the colonies in their struggle for liberty was unfortunate for the morals of the people. The soldiers, many of them, were unbelievers. French infidelity was, by them, spread far and wide.

The tendency of war is to lower the moral tone of the people engaging in it. The War of the Revolution was no exception to this tendency.

The people were exceedingly poor. They lived remote from each other. Because of their poverty, and the manner in which their homes were distributed, it was impossible for the people to possess and use the means of grace necessary to a healthy moral and spiritual tone.[1]

At the close of the Revolutionary War, so much had been spoken and written on the subject of liberty that multitudes of the people were practical anarchists. They did not believe in any kind of government. Mr. John Fiske, the historian, characterizes this as "The critical period in American history."

The people having freed themselves from the government of Great Britain, were now compelled to give attention to the formation of a suitable government for themselves and for their posterity. This matter must receive attention. But little time or thought could be given to religion.

Almost immediately after independence had been secured, difficulties with the mother country arose which culminated in the War of 1812.

The foregoing are some of the reasons for the deplorable condition of affairs described in the beginning of this chapter. And besides this, and worst of all, is a tendency belonging to man to turn from God. There was, however, a remnant in this dark period earnestly determined to serve God. Here and there a man in the ministry, as a true prophet, spoke for God.

REVIEW.
1. What is the subject of this chapter?
2. What was the religious condition in the United States during the early nineteenth century?
3. What was the moral and spiritual condition of the people?
4. What was the prevalent theological belief?

---

[1] By this, the author means that it was difficult—if not impossible—for these poor citizens to come together from such distances to have regular religious services, and the aid of a dedicated man of God. They could not afford a place of worship, could not find a Bible, nor could they afford the hiring of someone who knew the Scriptures to expound it to them.

5. What does Dr. Dorchester say on this point?
6. Give seven causes for the prevalent unbelief and immorality?
7. What is said of Sunday Schools, Bible societies, Missionary socie-ties, etc.?
8. What of the sectarian spirit among Christians?
9. Was the condition altogether bad?

Chapter Two

REACHING OUT AFTER BETTER THINGS

To realize one's lost estate is to begin to be saved. The man, or the community, is in a bad condition when he says: "I have need of nothing."

The General Assembly of the Presbyterian Church in 1798 issued a general letter which said: "Formidable innovations and convulsions in Europe threaten destruction to morals and religion. Scenes of devastation and bloodshed unparalleled in the history of modern nations have convulsed[1] the world, and our country is threatened with similar concomitants.[2] We perceive with pain and fearful apprehension a general dereliction[3] of religious principles and practice among our fellow-citizens; a visible and prevailing impiety and contempt for the laws and instructions of religion, and an abounding infidelity, which in many instances leads to atheism itself. The profligacy[4] and corruption of the public morals have advanced with a progress proportionate to the declension in religion. Profaneness, pride, luxury, injustice, intemper-

---

[1] Shaken.
[2] Circumstances.
[3] Decay.
[4] State of abandoning virtue, principles, and decency.

ance, lewdness, and every species of debauchery and loose indulgence greatly abound."

The Methodist Church, at a later period, expressed itself in a similar tone. These lamentations were favorable symptoms. There were, it is true, occasional revivals of religion in different portions of the country in the last years of the eighteenth century. They were, however, only local and temporary in their extent and influence. On the frontier, where the greatest deprivations were endured, and where also the people of God realized most fully their spiritual desolation, men began to call on God with intense faith and fervor.

The prayer of the Hebrew prophet was the burden of their cry: "O Lord, revive thy work in the midst of the years, in the midst of the years make known; in wrath remember mercy."[1] Christians entered into covenants with one another to spend specified portions of time in prayer for a spiritual awakening. After a time there began to be preaching, the specific aim of which was to turn men from sin to holiness. Two brothers name McGee—brothers in the flesh and in the Lord—in the last months of 1799 began to conduct meetings in some communities with very encouraging results. The fire which they kindled spread rapidly to remote parts of the country. The greatest of these revival meetings was held in August, 1801, at Cane Ridge in Bourbon County, Kentucky. It was here in which Barton W. Stone, a minister in the Presbyterian Church, was the most conspicuous figure. This meeting continued six or seven days and nights—and would have continued longer, but food for so great a multitude could not be found. It was estimated that from twenty to thirty thousand people attended.

The Rev. E. B. Crisman, in his "History of the Cumberland Presbyterian Church," says about the character of the preaching, "the ministers dwelt, with great power, continually on the necessity of repentance and faith, the fullness of the gospel for all, and the necessity of the

---

[1] Habakkuk 3:2

new birth. They eloquently and earnestly presented the purity and justice of God's law, the odious and destructive consequences of sin, and the freeness and sufficiency of pardon for all."

Some good men thought that this kind of preaching was calculated to injure the church. Charges of heresy were therefore preferred against the following named ministers in the Presbyterian Church: Richard McNemar,[1] John Thompson, John Dunlavy,[2] Robert Marshall, and Barton Warren Stone. The result was that they withdrew from the Synod by which they were being tried. They had no thought of leaving the Presbyterian denomination, but for the sake of peace they left the Synod. Instead of peace, though, they found themselves in the midst of such a war as they had never known before. They blamed their creed, the Westminster Confession of Faith, for the trouble in which they were involved. Because of this, they turned against all human authoritative creeds. They received the Bible—and nothing else—as the rule of their faith. Churches began to be organized called simply "Christian," with the Holy Scriptures alone as a sufficient statement of their belief and as an infallible guide in the way of righteousness.

There was dissatisfaction also in the Methodist Church and a desire for larger liberty. The Rev. James O'Kelly, of Virginia, was a member of the General Conference in 1792. He made an ineffectual effort to secure a modification of the power of the bishops in the appointment of preachers. He and his friends left the body. At first they were called "Republican Methodists;" but later the name "Christian" was taken and the Bible alone was received as a book of authority.

A man named Jones—Abner Jones—member of a regular Baptist Church, in Vermont, "had a peculiar travail of mind in regard to sec-

---

[1] McNemar stood fast for a time, and was the driving force behind the famous *Last Will and Testament of the Springfield Presbytery,* but within four years, he left the faith and joined the Shakers. More of his story can be found in *A Sketch of the Life and Labors of Richard McNemar,* available from Cobb Publishing (theCobbSix.com).
[2] John Dunlavy, along with his brother-in-law Richard McNemar, joined the Shakers in 1805.

tarian names and human creeds." In the year 1800 he gathered a small church in the town of Lyndon, Vermont, on the general principles named above. In 1802 a congregation was organized in Bradford, Vermont, on the Bible alone. In 1803 a similar organization came into existence in Piermont, New Hampshire. A Baptist Church in Portsmouth, same state, adopted similar views on the subject of creeds and names. In many parts of New England, New York, New Jersey, and Pennsylvania, human names and creeds were abandoned for the name "Christian" and the word of the Lord alone.

Influences were also at work on the other side of the Atlantic, which were destined to be powerful in the New World in aiding to secure a better faith and more Christ-like life. Thomas Campbell was a minister in the Presbyterian Church[1] in Ireland. He was grieved by the divisions in the church of his choice in Ireland and Scotland. He made earnest, but ineffectual, efforts to bring about union. His health failed, and in 1807 he came to the United States. Here he found the same sectarian spirit against which he had contended in Europe. Desiring to bring about cooperation in caring for the people in their spiritual destitution he organized "The Christian Association, of Washington, Pa." It failed to accomplish the purpose of its organization.

Alexander Campbell, a son of Thomas Campbell, came to America in 1809. He knew something of the grief of his father because of the divisions of the Presbyterian Church in Ireland and Scotland. For a year before he came to the United States, he had been in contact with and under the influence of the Haldanes, and others, in Scotland, who were dissatisfied with the sectarian divisions in the church and were earnestly seeking for "a more excellent way."[2] He was, therefore, prepared to sympathize with and enter into cooperation with his father in an effort to find a basis of peace and union for the children of God.

---

[1] Actually, part of the Seceder Presbyterian Church, a group that had split from the regular Presbyterian Church some years earlier.

[2] Among other things, the Haldanes insisted on weekly observance of the Lord's Supper.

This restlessness, and these desires for something better, in places so remote from each other, were born of the Spirit of God.

REVIEW.
1. What is the subject of this chapter?
2. What favorable condition is mentioned?
3. What did the General Assembly say in 1798?
4. What prayer began now to be offered?
5. With whom did the revival begin?
6. When and where reach its climax?
7. Who was the central figure?
8. What was the character of the preaching?
9. Who were charged with heresy?
10. Mention other movements looking to better things.
11. Who was prepared, and how, in a distant land for a great work in this?
12. The desire for something better originated with whom?

Chapter Three

THE PURPOSE

OF THE PIONEERS

The church was divided. The spirit of sectarianism was rampant. Among the people of God there was no cooperation in evangelistic work. Party was superior to Christ in the thoughts and efforts of multitudes that wore his name. The mission of the church, as a result, was not fulfilled. Men were passing into eternity without the good hope of everlasting life through Jesus Christ our Lord. The hearts of the men named in the last chapter were grieved. They were good men. Their bodies were temples of the Holy Spirit. They loved God. They loved men. For the salvation of the lost they had an earnest desire. They had learned from the Son of God that the union of believers must precede the conversion of the world. They learned this from his prayer in the seventeenth chapter of John. In this prayer Jesus said: "I do not pray for these alone, but also for those who will believe in Me through their word; that they all may be one, as You, Father, are in Me, and I in You; that they also may be one in Us, that the world may believe that You sent Me."[1]

It was for peace that Stone, McNemar, Dunlavy, Marshall and Thompson, withdrew from the Synod. They were ablaze with evangelistic fer-

---

[1] John 17:20-21. NKJV.

vor. They were prominent and enthusiastic in the work of the revival, recently inaugurated. They rejoiced to have the cooperation of their brethren in other churches. They were determined that this good work should continue. But this could not be if there was strife. To avoid this was their purpose in removing themselves from the oversight of the synod that was accusing them of neglecting, in their public ministry, the doctrines of the Standards—the Confession of Faith and the Catechisms. Peace, not war, was their purpose. Their desire was that peace might prevail, for the sake of him who died for them, and for the sake of souls in sin.

There was no thought of originating a denomination. From their point of view the number of denominations was already too great. The thought of another denomination did not enter their minds. The thought that they should, in any way, shape, or form be the agents in bringing into existence a religious party, would have caused them to experience a shudder of horror. They hated the sectarian spirit with a holy hatred. They condemned the spirit of division. The church of Christ at the beginning was one, and this was according to the mind of our Lord. The church ought now to be one. Why couldn't its members be joined together in the same mind and in the same judgment? Their purpose was union, not division —harmony, not discord.

As we have seen, Mr. Jones, in Vermont, "had a peculiar travail of mind in regard to sectarian names and human creeds." These names and creeds, he thought, divided the people of God. They, therefore, were in the way of the success of the gospel. It could not do its work in bringing men out of death into life. Sectarian names must then be repudiated by Christians. These names must be displaced by the names used in the New Testament to designate the disciples of Jesus. Human creeds, as terms of communion, must be discarded, that the divine creed—the creed of the church in the beginning—might occupy its legitimate place. This would certainly please Christ—the Head of the Body. The repudiation of human names and creeds, and the adoption of New Testament names, and the primitive creed, would promote union and so hasten the conversion of the world.

"The O'Kelly secession," as it is known in Methodist church history, was, at the first, only a protest against the authority of the bishops in the location of preachers. There was on the part of Mr. O'Kelly and his friends a desire for greater liberty—a liberty to which they believed they were entitled according to the teaching of the New Testament. The Methodist name and the Methodist "Articles of Religion," were therefore discarded for the name "Christian," and for the New Testament as the only book possessing authority in religious faith and life. The faces of all the men here named, and others associated with them, were turned in the same direction—toward the Christ and his word—and this in the interest of peace and union.

Thomas Campbell possessed the same pacific spirit and earnest desire. He struggled and worked in the interest of peace and union in his own unfortunate denomination before he left Ireland. In the United States he manifested the same spirit. His standing in the Presbytery of Chartiers, of which he was a member, was seriously imperiled by an invitation which he extended to pious men and women of other denominations to participate in the celebration of the Lord's Supper.[1] He organized "The Christian Association of Washington, Pa." to secure the co-operation of Christians regardless of denominational connection, in ministering to the spiritually destitute.

His address to the Associated Synod of North America when he was on trial for extending an invitation to Christ-like men and women to participate in our Lord's memorial feast of love contains the following language: "How great the injustice, to thrust out from communion a Christian brother, a fellow minister, for saying and doing none other things than those which our divine Lord and his holy apostles have taught, and enjoined[2] to be spoken and done by his ministering servants, and to be received and observed by his people!" ... "Saying and doing the very same things that are said and done before our eyes on

---

[1] He was accused of heresy by the Seceder Presbyterian Church for serving other Presbyterians—not from the Seceder branch—the Lord's Supper.

[2] Required.

the sacred page is infallibly right, as well as all-sufficient for the edification of the church." He declared that the course pursued by him appeared "indispensably necessary to promote and secure the unity, peace, and purity of the church." "Say brethren," he exclaimed, "what is my offence, that I should be thrust out from the heritage of the Lord, or from serving him in that good work to which he has been graciously pleased to call me?"

REVIEW.
1. What was the purpose of the pioneers?
2. Why did Stone and others withdraw from the Synod?
3. Why give up denominational names and creeds?
4. For what was Thomas Campbell tried?
5. His address exhibits what kind of a spirit?

Chapter Four

THE DECLARATION AND ADDRESS

Soon after the organization of "The Christian Association of Washington" in 1809, to which reference has already been made, a committee was appointed to prepare a statement for the public. Thomas Campbell was a member of this committee, and wrote the address. This was designed to set forth to the public, in a clear and definite manner, the object of the movement in which he and those associated with him were engaged. This document proved to be a *declaration of independence* and it possesses, in the history of Christianity in the United States—especially in the history of the disciples of Christ—great value. Alexander Campbell said, in 1861, that "it contains what may be called the embryo, or the rudiments, of a great and rapidly increasing community; ... the elements of a great movement of vital interest to every citizen of Christ's kingdom."

It was given to the world under the title of "A Declaration and Address." It contained "a preamble and resolutions." The preamble declared that "it is high time for us not only to think, but also to act for ourselves; ... and to take all our measures directly and immediately from the Divine Standard." "The sole purpose" of the Association was declared to be "to promote simple evangelical Christianity." Each member was to pay a specified sum of money "to support a pure gospel ministry, that shall reduce to practice that whole form of doctrine, worship, discipline and government, expressly revealed and enjoined in the Word of God; and also for supplying the poor with the Holy Scriptures."

Article IV declared that

> "this society by no means considers itself a church, nor does, at all, assume to itself the powers peculiar to such a society ... but merely as voluntary advocates of church reformation." The members of the society agree to "support such ministers ... as exhibit a manifest conformity to the original standard, in conversation and doctrine, in zeal and diligence; only such as reduce to practice that simple, original form of Christianity expressly exhibited upon the sacred page, without attempting to inculcate anything of human authority, of private opinion, or inventions of men, as having any place in the constitution, faith or worship of the Christian Church, or anything as matter of Christian faith or duty, for which there cannot be produced a 'Thus saith the Lord,' either in express terms or by approved precedent."

Thomas Campbell was accustomed to saying: "We make our appeal to the law and to the testimony. Whatever is not found therein we must of course abandon." This was his reply to his son Alexander when he suggested that the principles of "The Declaration and Address" required them to give up the practice of infant baptism, since for it there was neither precept nor example in the Scriptures. It was in a discussion of the principles of "The Declaration and Address" that Thomas Campbell uttered the words which have the force of an axiom among the disciples: "*WHERE THE SCRIPTURES SPEAK, WE SPEAK; AND WHERE THE SCRIPTURES ARE SILENT, WE ARE SILENT.*" It is said that "a solemn silence pervaded the assembly" when Thomas Campbell uttered these words. Dr. Richardson, the biographer of Alexander

Campbell, says that "never before had religious duty been presented to them in so simple a form. Never before had the great principles on which this religious enterprise rested been so clearly presented to their minds."

It was believed by Mr. Campbell and his friends, that this pregnant saying was "decisive of all religious strifes and of all distressing doubts." Dr. Richardson says that "it was from the moment when these significant words were uttered and accepted that the more in- telligent ever afterward dated the formal and actual commencement of the Reformation." The principles involved in this simple rule were far-reaching and revolutionary. Some didn't have the courage to apply them and ceased to walk with those who sought a better foundation for their religious life and work.

Instead of *Reformation* the principle meant *Restoration*—a return to the Christianity of Christ as it was at the first, and as it is described in the New Testament. Thomas Campbell, himself, did not understand the radical character of his proposition, but he was a man of courage and faithfully applied it in the determination of all questions of faith and duty. Its faithful application led him to abandon the baptism of infants and the practice of pouring as a form of baptism. The Scrip- tures do not speak of these customs. For them there is neither precept nor example in the Bible.

In the "Address" accompanying the "Declaration" the evils of division are lamented. The hope is expressed that the brethren in all the churches would cooperate in an effort to "resume that original unity, peace, and purity" which belonged to the church in the days of the apostles. To do this it is only necessary "to conform to the model and adopt the practice of the primitive church, expressly exhibited in the New Testament." Attention was called to the fact that the churches already "agreed in the great doctrines of faith and holiness," and also "as to the positive ordinances of gospel institution, so that," the disa- greements were "about the things in which the kingdom of God does not consist; that is, about matters of private opinion."

The members of the various denominations are addressed as "dear brethren" and are assured "of our esteem and love." Nothing was further from the purpose of the "Christian Association" than to make "a new creed or standard for the church." The propositions submitted, it was expressly declared, were not "to be made a term of communion." "Nothing," said their authors, "can be further from our intention." "Creeds and confessions," they said, are opposed "only in so far as they oppose the unity of the church." "It is the abuse and not the lawful use of such compilations that we oppose," is language found in the appendix to "The Declaration and Address." And the following words deserve to be written in letters of gold: "Our intention, therefore, with respect to all the churches of Christ is perfectly amicable. We heartily wish their reformation, but by no means their hurt or confusion."

REVIEW.
1. When was the Declaration and Address written?
2. Where?
3. By whom was the Christian Association organized?
4. Who prepared the Declaration and Address?
5. What did Alexander Campbell say about it?
6. Was the Christian Association a church?
7. What was its aim?
8. What axiom is here quoted?
9. What was lamented in the Declaration and Address?
10. How far were creeds opposed?
11. Could the address, or any part of it, be made a test of fellowship?
12. What was the attitude of the Association toward the denominations?

Chapter Five

REFORMATIONS AND RESTORATION

"The heart is deceitful above all things and desperately wicked." Men are "by nature children of wrath."[1] Even Paul found that to live the life of a Christian required a constant effort. He said: "With me, who would do good, evil is present."[2] He expressed a fear that after having preached the Gospel to others, he himself would be rejected.[3] Concerning the church he predicted a "falling away." He spoke of one who would sit in the temple of God claiming to be God.[4] He said that the time would come when men would "not endure sound teaching," but would heap to themselves "teachers after their own lusts," that they would turn away their ears from the truth, and turn aside unto fables."[5] When he wrote his second Epistle to the church in Thessalonica he said, "The mystery of lawlessness is already at work."[6] John said that in his day "many false prophets" had "gone out into the world."[7]

---

[1] Ephesians 2:3
[2] Romans 7:21
[3] 1 Corinthians 9:27
[4] 2 Thessalonians 2:3-4
[5] 2 Timothy 4:3-4
[6] 2 Thessalonians 2:7
[7] 1 John 4:1

In the Jewish Church, described in the Old Testament, there were apostasies and reformations. Great reformations originated and were carried forward under Josiah, Hezekiah, and Ezra. In the experience of the church of Christ the predictions of Paul have been fulfilled: There have been apostasies. Great corruptions in faith and life have, at different times, characterized the Christian Church. These have made reformations necessary. From the sixth to the sixteenth centuries the teaching of our Lord was greatly perverted, and the life of the church was very unlike the life that the Christ desires.

This made necessary the reformation of the sixteenth century under Martin Luther. At three points there was reformation under the leadership of this great man:

(1) Men were taught that there is "one mediator also between God and men, himself man, Christ Jesus."[1] The priest then is not necessary in order to acceptably approach God. Jesus is the "High Priest of our profession."[2] He himself said: "No one comes unto the Father, but by me."[3] "He is able to save to the uttermost them that draw near unto God through him."[4] Men do not, therefore, need the mediation of Mary, the mother of Jesus, nor of saints, nor of angels.

(2) The Word of God was given to the people in their own tongue, and they were encouraged to read it. The Word, previous to this Reformation, was in a language with which the people were not acquainted. Its entrance into the minds of the people illuminated their understandings and brought them into a new life.

(3) Men were taught by the reformer that they are justified by faith in Jesus Christ and not by works of merit. The apostate church had taught that in works there is merit and that by them men are justified.

---

[1] 1 Timothy 2:5
[2] Hebrews 3:1
[3] John 14:6
[4] Hebrews 7:25

John Calvin, in Switzerland, at the same time, affirmed with great power that God alone is Sovereign. Men are dependent on and accountable to him, and to no other. The reformers of the sixteenth century affirmed with "Peter and the apostles" that "we must obey God rather than men."[1]

There were reformers before the Reformation; protestants before the day of Protestantism. Their protests, however, were apparently in vain. Their attempted reformations were futile. John Wycliffe, in England, was one of the most important of these men and represented one of the most important of these efforts to bring the church to a better faith and purer life. Those who were in sympathy with him were called "Lollards." They were diligent in going about teaching the people. The ambition of Wycliffe, who has been called the "Morning Star of the Reformation," was to give the Bible to the people of Great Britain in their own language. The work of Wycliffe and "the Lollards" prepared the way for a more Scriptural belief and holier life, when the time came. The Reformation in England was not so violent, nor revolutionary in character, as on the continent of Europe. The work of John Knox, in Scotland, was in harmony with the reformation inaugurated by Luther.

In the early part of the eighteenth century the church in England had become cold and formal. The forms of godliness were observed, but there was a lack of power. The Wesleys—John and Charles—therefore, inaugurated a reformation, the key note of which was "Personal holiness." Their effort was to bring the church back to the Christly life. Each attempt to purge the Body of Christ of doctrinal and practical errors and to bring in an era of purer faith and more consecrated living was an improvement on its predecessors.

The faces of the reformers were turned in the right direction. They looked toward the Christ. Each was a step out of darkness into light. They made possible the work in which the disciples are engaged.

---

[1] Acts 5:30

There is this marked difference, however, in the movement inaugurated by B. W. Stone, Thomas Campbell, Alexander Campbell, Walter Scott, and other holy men who wrought with them, and the reformations preceding. The work of the men here named and the work of the disciples of Christ is **Restoration**, rather than Reformation. Their position was, and ours is, to go back to the Christ and his apostles that we may learn from him and them what to believe and do, in order to please God and secure eternal life. Nothing of this kind had ever been attempted. The real remedy for existing evils in the church is to go back to the beginning and build anew on the one Divine foundation. They would build "upon the foundation of apostles and prophets, Christ Jesus himself being the Chief Corner Stone."[1] "Other foundation can no man lay," with the Divine approval, for the church, "than that which is laid, which is Jesus Christ."[2] Restoration, therefore, rather than Reformation is the work of the disciples of Christ. To believe and do no other things than those enjoined by the Christ and his ambassadors cannot be wrong—must be infallibly right, and altogether safe.

REVIEW.
1. What is the subject of this chapter?
2. What was predicted concerning the Church?
3. What was the experience of the Jewish Church?
4. What made necessary the reformation of the church of Christ?
5. By whom and when inaugurated?
6. Mention the three points gained by Luther?
7. Name other reformers?
8. What was proposed by Stone and the Campbells?
9. In what does it differ from mere reformation?

---

[1] Ephesians 2:20
[2] 1 Corinthians 3:11

Chapter Six

THE PROCESS OF DISCOVERY

The aim was the restoration of the faith, the ordinances, and the life of the church as they were before the falling away predicted by Paul. The constant appeal was to the word of the Lord in the New Testament. "Nothing," it was said, "ought to be received into the faith or be made a term of communion among Christians, that is not as old as the New Testament."

"Inferences and deduction from Scripture premises were not to be considered as binding" upon the consciences of Christians further than they perceive the connection. "No such deductions can be made terms of communion," they said, "but do properly belong to the ... progressive edification of the church." In cases where means are necessary to the observance of ordinances not expressly revealed in Scripture, they may be adopted and used as "human expedients, without any pretense to a more sacred origin, so that any subsequent alteration or difference in the observance of these things might produce no contention or division in the church."

There was no serious dissatisfaction on the part of the promoters of this movement with the orthodox conception of the Christian religion. Their purpose was practical rather than doctrinal. But the fundamental principle adopted in the beginning and clearly stated in the Declaration and Address, with its accompanying Appendix, steadfastly adhered to, led necessarily to important discoveries and changes.

The New Testament makes the fact clear, for instance, that divisions are sinful.[1] Nor is there authority for denominational names. Their tendency is to foster the party spirit and perpetuate the sin of schism. The people of God ought, therefore, to be known only by the names applied to them in the New Testament. Jesus taught that all are brethren. There is no warrant, therefore, for dividing the disciples into clergy and laity.

A study of the Scriptures led to the conviction that only those who believe in Jesus and confess him before men are entitled to baptism. The good men, called of God to inaugurate this movement for a return in faith and in life to the Christianity of Christ, soon saw that, in New Testament times, baptism was administered where there was much water,[2] that the persons baptized went into the water,[3] and that in baptism there was a burial, and a resurrection.[4] Having only had water sprinkled on their foreheads, in infancy, they discovered that they had not been baptized. They therefore were immersed.

They discovered, also, that baptism is much more than a mere form; a ceremony to be observed in order to become a member of the Church. It was seen to be an act of self-surrender to the Lord Jesus. It is an act in which the baptized enters into a covenant with the Son of God, to be and to do whatever he would like him to be and to do. It, therefore, occupies a prominent and important place in the way of salvation.

Even before this discovery it was seen that the disciples, under the ministry of the Apostles, and with their approval, came together on

---

[1] Galatians 5:16-21
[2] John 3:23
[3] Mark 1:5, 10; Acts 8:38
[4] Romans 6:4; Colossians 2:12

the first day of the week to break bread[1] in memory of their Redeemer. The principle to which they had bound themselves enabled them to see that the central truth of the New Testament, the central truth of the Bible, the truth of the Christian system, in an important sense the creed of Christianity, is that Jesus is the Christ, the Son of God. Soon a practical use of this truth was made in evangelistic work. All who declared that they believed this in the heart were, without delay, admitted to baptism. They also discovered that faith is produced by hearing the Word of Christ,[2] and that the steps to be taken in order to have assurance of forgiveness are (1) hearing, (2) believing, (3) repenting, (4) confessing Christ, (5) and baptism, in the name of the Lord Jesus, and into the name of the Father, and of the Son, and of the Holy Spirit. Their determination was to "keep close by the observance of all Divine ordinances, after the example of the primitive church, exhibited in the New Testament."

For a short time some practiced the washing of feet as a religious ordinance. It seems that Jesus made stronger statements about washing one another's feet than he made concerning baptism. He said: "If I do not wash you, you have no part with me." "If I, then, your Lord and Master, have washed your feet, you also ought to wash one another's feet." "I have given you an example, that you should do as I have done to you."[3] Why, then, do the Disciples not do this as a religious rite? They attempt to follow "the example of the primitive church, exhibited in the New Testament," and there is no "example" of washing one another's feet as a religious ordinance. Did Jesus intend to establish an ordinance by the language above quoted? The Apostles and early Christians did not think so. Their conduct is of great value to us in our effort to understand the mind of the Master. The Apostles understood that Jesus intended to establish religious ordinances in what he said concerning baptism and the Supper of the Lord.

---

[1] Acts 20:7
[2] Romans 10:17
[3] John 13:8, 14-15

The church in the Apostolic age ministered to the necessities of the saints.[1] This custom made it necessary to appoint men to "serve tables."[2] Such men are called deacons. The great work committed to the church by its Head, Jesus Christ our Lord, is the preaching of the gospel. Evangelists were, therefore, in the primitive church—men who went from place to place publishing the good news.[3] It is necessary that the spiritual life should be tenderly cared for. There must, to this end, be bishops, deacons, teachers. These were in the primitive church,[4] and they ought to be in the church at the present time.

Thus we see the value of the principle, the manner of its application, and how in the process of discovery it led and restrained the men who committed themselves to it.

REVIEW.
1. This chapter describes what?
2. What was the aim of Stone, the Campbells, and their associates?
3. Was their purpose doctrinal or practical?
4. What led to important doctrinal divergences?
5. Name the things discovered by a study of the New Testament.
6. Why practice baptism and not the washing of feet as a religious ordinance?
7. Name the church officers and why they exist.
8. By this study what do we see?

---

[1] Acts 2:44-45; 4:32, 34-37;5:1-11;11:27-30; 1 Corinthians 16:1-2
[2] Acts 6:1-7
[3] Acts 21:8; 8:5-26; 2 Timothy 4:5
[4] Acts 20:28; 1 Timothy 2:1-7; Titus 1:5-9; 1 Peter 5:1-4

Chapter Seven

THE UNITY OF THE CHURCH

The Declaration and Address affirmed that

> "the Church of Christ upon earth is essentially, intentionally and constitutionally one; consisting of all those in every place that profess their faith in Christ and obedience to him in all things according to the Scriptures, and that manifest the same by their tempers and conduct; and of none else, as none else can be truly and properly called Christians."

Paul also affirms that the body of Christ, the church, "is one, and hath many members,"[1] He likens the church to the human body in which the feet, ears, eyes, hands, head, etc., are integral parts. These members are so closely united that "when one member suffers, all the members suffer with it; or when one member is honored, all the members rejoice with it." So also is the body of Christ, "intentionally and constitutionally."[2]

To cause a schism in the church is a great sin. "Heresies," or parties, are placed by Paul among "the works of the flesh." The sin of schism stands with "fornication, uncleanness, lasciviousness, idolatry, sorcery, enmities, strife, jealousies, wraths, factions, envyings, drunkenness,

---

[1] 1 Corinthians 12:12
[2] 1 Corinthians 12:12-27

revellings, and such like."[1] "Divisions and heresies" are also words found in this enumeration of "the works of the flesh." So great a sin is it to cause "factions, divisions, heresies" that Paul says: "They which practice such things shall not inherit the kingdom of God."[2] In his Epistle to the Romans he says: "Mark them which are causing the divisions and occasions of stumbling, contrary to the doctrine which you learned; and turn away from them. For," he continues, "they that are such serve not our Lord Christ, but their own belly; and by their smooth and fair speech they beguile the hearts of the innocent."[3]

Word came to Paul that there were "contentions" and "divisions" in the Church in Corinth.[4] The members of the church were saying: "I am of Paul; and I of Apollos; and I of Cephas."[5] He tells them that their "contentions" and "divisions" are evidences of carnality.[6] These are of "the works of the flesh;" no part of "the fruit of the spirit."[7]

The late John A. Broadus, D.D., of the Southern Baptist Theological Seminary, characterized the Epistle to the Ephesians as "An Essay on Christian Union." The heart of this essay, he said, is the fourth chapter. In that place the apostle beseeches "the saints which are at Ephesus," "to walk worthily of the calling wherewith ye were called, with all lowliness and meekness, with long-suffering, forbearing one another in love; giving diligence to keep the unity of the Spirit in the bond of peace."[8] He then gives seven reasons why they should live together in this manner. "You are," he seems to say,

(1) "members of one body, the church (Col. 1:18);

---

[1] Galatians 5:19-21
[2] Galatians 5:21
[3] Romans 16:17-18
[4] 1 Corinthians 1:10-11
[5] 1 Corinthians 1:12
[6] 1 Corinthians 3:1-3
[7] Galatians 5:22-23
[8] Ephesians 4:1-3

(2) animated by one Spirit, the Holy Spirit (Rom. 8:9-11);

(3) sustained by one hope, the hope of eternal life through Jesus Christ (I Peter 1:3-5);

(4) hold fast to the one faith, the faith of the Son of God (Gal. 2:20);

(5) have passed through the one baptism, an immersion in water in the name of the Lord Jesus and into the name of the Father, and of the Son and of the Holy Spirit (Acts 8:38- 39; Acts 10:47, 48; Rom. 6:4; Col. 2:12; Matt. 28:19-20);

(6) you are obedient to the one Lord, even Jesus Christ (Acts 10:36), and

(7) recognizes 'one God and Father of all, who is over all, and through all and in all.'" "Because of these things that you experience and hold in common 'I ... beseech you to walk worthily,'" etc. (Eph. 4:1-13).

Jesus spoke of his church as a unit. He said: "I will build my *church*,"[1] not church**es**. Paul says that "Christ loved the *church*,"[2] not church**es**, "and gave himself for *it*," not *them*. To the Jews the Son of Man said: "And other sheep I have, which are not of this fold; them also I must bring, and they shall hear my voice; and they shall become one flock, one Shepherd."[3] The Christ, by his death on the cross, took away "the law of commandments contained in ordinances," the law of Moses, "that he might create in himself of the two," Jews and Gentiles, "one new man," or church, and that he "might reconcile them both," Gentiles and Jews, "in one body."[4]

Jesus prayed for the unity of his people: "Holy Father," he said, "keep them in Your name which You have given Me, that they may be one,

---

[1] Matthew 16:18
[2] Ephesians 5:25
[3] John 10:16
[4] Ephesians 2:13-18

even as we are."[1] And this prayer was answered. "The multitude of them that believed were of one heart and soul."[2] He prayed also "for them that believe on me through their word;" the word of the Apostles, "that they may all be one; even as You Father, are in Me, and I in You, that they also may be in Us." Why? "That the world may believe that You did send me."[3] And this prayer will be answered. Jesus said at the grave of Lazarus: "You hear me always."[4] Our divisions must disappear. They are displeasing to the Head of the body. The church ought to be, must be, will be, one as it was in the beginning.

Paul gives the basis of unity and union. In his first Epistle to the Corinthians he discusses this problem and says: "Another foundation" for the church, "no man can lay than that which is laid, which is Jesus Christ."[5] As a building, the church rests on the Christ. He is also the magnet by which men are drawn together. "And I, if I be lifted up from the earth, will draw all men unto myself."[6] As men are drawn toward the Son of God, they are drawn toward one another. And herein is the solution of the current problem concerning the unity of the church.

REVIEW.
1. This chapter treats of what subject?
2. Quote the Declaration and Address on the oneness of the church.
3. What does Paul say on this subject, and where?
4. What does he say about divisions among Christians?
5. What part of the New Testament speaks especially of union?
6. Outline the argument in Ephesians 4:1-6.
7. How did Jesus speak of his church?
8. For what did Jesus pray?

---

[1] John 17:11
[2] Acts 4:32
[3] John 17:20-21
[4] John 11:42
[5] 1 Corinthians 3:11
[6] John 12:32

9. Who, in the New Testament, gives the basis of union, and what is it?
10. What solution of the union problem is last mentioned in this chapter?

Chapter Eight

THE GOSPEL CONDITIONS OF PARDON

Walter Scott was one of the most interesting men engaged in this effort to restore primitive Christianity. He was a Scotchman, and well-educated. In faith, when he came to the United States, he was a Presbyterian. He had been in this country but a short time before he became acquainted with the Campbells and their friends. He at once became interested in their movement. He was, in a short time, enlisted in the cause. As a student and preacher he was warm, enthusiastic, and bold. He dared to think, and thinking, dared to speak. He soon discovered and exhibited the central truth of the Christian system—the truth that Jesus is the Christ, the Son of the living God. His investigations led him in 1827, in New Lisbon, Ohio, to present, for the first time, the conditions of pardon as they are now preached by the Disciples of Christ. They were gathered from the great commission which is recorded by Matthew, Mark, Luke and John as follows:

> "All authority has been given to me in heaven and on earth. Go, therefore, and make disciples of all the nations, baptizing them into the name of the Father and of the Son and of the Holy Spirit: teaching them to observe all things, whatever I commanded you; and be-

hold, I am with you always, even unto the end of the age." (Matt. 28:18-20).

"You go into all the world, and preach the gospel to the whole creation. He that believes and is baptized shall be saved; but he that disbelieves shall be condemned." (Mark 16:15-16).

"And he said to them, thus it is written, that the Christ should suffer and rise again from the dead on the third day; and that repentance and remission of sins should be preached in his name unto all the nations beginning at Jerusalem." (Luke 24:46-47).

"As the Father has sent me, even so send I you. And when he had said this, he breathed on them, and said to them, Receive the Holy Spirit: whoever's sins you forgive they are forgiven to them; whoever's sins you retain, they are retained." (John 20:21-23).

Mr. Scott quickly saw that the following items are in these last words of the Master to his disciples:

(1) Go
(2) preach
(3) belief
(4) repentance
(5) baptism
(6) salvation
(7) the Holy Spirit
(8) condemnation if rejected.

The proclamation that the Christ commanded his friends to preach "to the whole creation" seemed to teach that, in order to have an assurance of salvation, men must hear, believe, repent, and be baptized. This proclamation also teaches that those who, hearing, refuse to believe and to become submissive to the authority of the Christ, shall be condemned. This seems to be the natural arrangement of the various items contained in the great commission. Mr. Scott began to preach the "way of salvation" as he believed his Lord would have him present it. Intense interest and great excitement resulted. The exposition of this royal proclamation was novel. The people had never heard anything like it. All ministers of the word claim this commission as the warrant for their work. But the Pedo-Baptists arrange the items in the following order:

(1) Go
(2) baptize
(3) preach
(4) repent
(5) believe
(6) salvation
(7) the Holy Spirit.

Baptism was, and is, administered by Pedo-Baptists to those who cannot believe and repent.

The Baptists, in practice, arrange the items of the commission in the following order:

(1) Go
(2) preach
(3) repent
(4) belief
(5) salvation
(6) the Holy Spirit
(7) baptism.

Mr. Scott saw that the book of Acts of Apostles is, in an important sense, a commentary, or exposition, of these last words of Jesus. The book of Acts shows in what way these friends of the Teacher understood him when he commanded them to go and "make disciples of all the nations." He, therefore, studied carefully this portion of the New

Testament in order to rightly understand the proclamation of salvation that Jesus commanded his followers to make.

It was not at all difficult to see that the men who received the command went out and preached. They proclaimed the gospel, and nothing else. Men heard, and as a result believed—believed that the message was from God and was true. Having received the message as true, the hearers were commanded to repent and be baptized for the remission of sins.[1] In all the cases of conversion described in the book of Acts this order is observed. There is not a single exception. In not a single case were persons baptized who were not believers, nor was one assured of pardon before baptism.

The above was seen to be the law of pardon for those who were led to accept the Son of God as their Savior. Having obtained an assurance of forgiveness, in the way above indicated, if we sin against God, the conditions of pardon are repentance and prayer.[2] When his children sin against one another they are required, in order to obtain pardon, to confess their faults, and ask the one against whom they have sinned for forgiveness.[3]

We are all guilty before God.[4] Because of his love for us, forgiveness is tendered on these easy and reasonable conditions. To refuse to submit to these simple terms graciously tendered by our Father, in infinite love, and thus spurn the offer of forgiveness, is madness.

REVIEW.
1. Who first in modern times preached the conditions of salvation as they are now presented by the Disciples of Christ?
2. When?
3. Where?
4. Quote the commission of Christ as given in the four Gospels.

---

[1] Acts 2:21-38
[2] Acts 8:22
[3] James 5:16; Luke 17:3-4
[4] Romans 2:9-20

5. What items are in it?
6. Name them as arranged by Pedo-Baptists.
7. In what way do the Baptists arrange them?
8. What is the New Testament arrangement as seen in the book of Acts?
9. This is the law of pardon for whom?
10. What is the law of forgiveness for Christians when they sin?
11. From whom and why this offer of pardon?

Chapter Nine

THE EVILS OF HUMAN CREEDS

Disciples have always opposed human authoritative creeds as tests of fellowship. The word "authoritative" is an important word in this connection. Alexander Campbell said:

> "By an authoritative human creed is meant an abstract of human opinions concerning the supposed cardinal articles of Christian faith, which summary is made a bond of union or term of communion." (*Millennial Harbinger*, 1832, p. 344).

They do not object to publishing what they understand to be the teaching of Holy Scripture on any subject of faith or duty as a matter of information. Their protest is against using such statements as a condition of fellowship. Mr. Campbell made such a statement in the *Millennial Harbinger* in 1846. Isaac Errett made such a statement concerning the teaching of the Disciples in the *Christian Standard*, and this is now published as a tract with the title, "Our Position." It is widely circulated and generally endorsed by the Disciples. But neither these statements, nor any others of human origin, can properly be used as tests of fellowship. The test propounded by Jesus is this:

"What think ye of Christ? Whose Son is he?"[1]

1. *Human creeds are destitute of Divine authority*. There is no command in Scripture to *make* them. There is no permission, even, in the Living Oracles to *have* or to *use* them.

2. *Their tendency has been to cast men who were earnest, and of an inquiring habit of mind, out of the church*. The reformers who were men of mental independence and honesty were condemned as heretics and cast out of the fellowship of the church by the influence of creeds.

3. *Their tendency is to displace Christ and his Word*. Men are commanded to hear him.[2] He, and he alone, is the Head of the body, the church.[3] He possesses all authority.[4] He is the Author and Finisher of the faith.[5] To substitute any other person or thing for him and his teaching, even by implication, is wrong. Anything, the tendency of which looks in that direction, is worthy of condemnation. The Son of God ought at all times, in all places, and in all things, to have the preeminence.

4. *Human authoritative creeds are not in harmony with such language as is found in the Word of God*, such as the following: "Hold the pattern of sound words which you have heard from me, in faith and love which is in Christ Jesus."[6] "Contend earnestly for the faith which was once for all delivered unto the saints."[7] "Stand fast, and hold the traditions which you were taught, whether by word, or by epistle of ours."[8] "This is my beloved Son; hear him."[9] These, and other similar

---

[1] Matthew 22:32
[2] Matthew 17:5
[3] Colossians 1:18
[4] Matthew 28:18
[5] Hebrews 12:2
[6] 2 Timothy 1:13
[7] Jude 3
[8] 2 Thessalonians 2:15
[9] Matthew 17:5

passages, clearly inhibit all rivals to the sacred writings; all substitutes, even by implication, for the New Testament teaching; all authoritative summaries of Christian doctrine. If men are commanded to hear Jesus Christ, as the ultimate authority, it is certain that a rival will not be tolerated.

5. *From the beginning of the church on Pentecost in Jerusalem, for at least two hundred years, there were no uninspired statements of belief possessing authority*. And this was the most harmonious, united, prosperous, and happy period of the church. When men began to construct doctrinal statements to be used as tests of fellowship, the period of controversy and division was inaugurated. The purest state and the most practical and useful, was when the church had "The One Book," and only the teaching of the Apostles, as authoritative.

6. *Human creeds are unfavorable to the development of spirituality*. No one was ever turned to God by a theological statement. Such statements not only fail to make Christians, but they do not promote sanctification. Compared with the life-inspiring statements of the Bible, they are but mummies. Admitting that they contain truth they are, at best, but skeletons of the truth contained in the Word of the Lord, and no one ever fell in love with a skeleton.

7. *They detract from the honor that belongs to the Holy Spirit, by assuming to be plainer and more intelligible than the Bible*. The Holy Spirit is the author of the Bible statements of saving and sanctifying truth. Paul says that an angel is not to be believed if he presumes to present something better than the Gospel of Christ.[1]

It has been said in their behalf that they are needed to keep heretics and other evil people out of the church. But there were heretics and wicked men in the church in the days of the Apostles—men who spoke and wrote under the special influence of the Holy Spirit. They apparently never thought of any other rule than the Gospel. Jude com-

---

[1] Galatians 1:6-9

plained that ungodly men, men who denied the one God and our Lord Jesus Christ, had crept into the church.[1] Paul speaks of "false brethren ... who came in secretly to spy out our liberty which we have in Christ Jesus, that they might bring us into bondage."[2] There were those who "went out from us because they were not of us,"[3] and there was Demas, who "forsook" Paul in the hour of danger, "having loved this present world."[4] Then there was Simon, the sorcerer;[5] Alexander, the coppersmith, who did Paul "much evil";[6] Phygellus and Hermogenes, who "turned away from" Paul;[7] Hymeneus and Alexander,[8] whom Paul delivered over to Satan. Judaizing teachers disturbed the peace of the church.[9] Some denied the resurrection.[10] Others said that the resurrection was past.[11] Teachers denied that Jesus had come in the flesh.[12]

Inspired men in the midst of these corruptions of Christianity did not draw up skillfully arranged articles of belief to preserve the purity of the church. Why should we? They adhered to the gospel and a simple confession of faith in Jesus as the Son of God. Why should not we be content with these?

REVIEW.
1. What is an important word in our discussion of human creeds?
2. Give Alexander Campbell's definition.
3. What points are made against creeds as here defined?
4. When did the church possess greatest unity and power?

---

[1] Jude 4

[2] Galatians 2:4

[3] 1 John 2:19

[4] 2 Timothy 4:10

[5] Acts 8:9-24

[6] 2 Timothy 4:14

[7] 2 Timothy 1:15

[8] 1 Timothy 1:20

[9] Acts 15:1-5

[10] 1 Corinthians 15;12

[11] 2 Timothy 2:18

[12] 1 John 4:1-3

5. Name some of the evils in the Apostolic Church.
6. What was the conduct of inspired men in their presence?
7. To what alone did they adhere?

Chapter Ten

THE EXALTATION OF THE CHRIST

Alexander Proctor said:

> Put Christ in your temple and whatever ought not to be there will depart at his bidding. Is your congregation disturbed by the presence of birds and beasts that defile it? Open the door to him and give him full possession, for he alone has power to drive them out. Is the temple of your heart infested with the beasts of selfishness, which show their presence in the works of the flesh? You cannot expel them by your will alone. Put Christ in your temple.

> There are yet those who are vainly trying to cleanse the temple of its falsehood by a scourge of small cords of doctrine spun out of their own brain. ... There are not wanting those who are seeking to cleanse their own lives by their law-keeping in their own strength. Put Christ in your temples, and whatever ought not to be there he will drive out.

This language well expresses our thought as to the place and power properly belonging to our Lord Jesus Christ. He is "the Alpha and the

Omega, the first and the last the beginning and the end."[1] "He is the image of the invisible God. … In Him were all things created, in the heavens and upon the earth, things visible and things invisible, whether thrones or dominions or principalities or powers; all things have been created through him, and for him; and he is before all things, and in him all things consist," or hold together. Possessing this peerless character he ought "in all things" to "have the pre-eminence."[2] When the Christ is given, in our thoughts and teaching, the place to which he is entitled, the schisms, contentions, strifes, and alienations, which among professed Christians hinder the Gospel in its regenerating work, will disappear.

With the disciples of Christ his divinity is more than a mere item of doctrine—it is the central truth of the gospel. It is the fundamental truth of the Christian religion. The one great purpose of gospel preaching is to persuade men to believe in, to love, and to obey Jesus. If men can be persuaded to enthrone Christ in their affections, to make him the Lord of their consciences, he will bring them to entertain right thoughts and to stand in right relations with everything else. The great need in the church and in the world is the exaltation of the Son of God.

He is called, in the New Testament, "the Son of God." He is so called because he was begotten of the Holy Spirit and born of the Virgin Mary. Hear these words:

> And the angel answered and said unto her, "The Holy Spirit shall come upon you, and the power of the Most High shall overshadow you. THEREFORE also that which is to be born shall be called holy, the Son of God" (Luke 1:35).

---

[1] Revelation 22:13
[2] Colossians 1:14-18

The Angel Gabriel used this language to "Mary, of whom was born Jesus, who is called Christ." (Matt. 1:16).

Jesus "was born of the seed of David according to the flesh," and "was declared to be the Son of God with power, according to the spirit of holiness, by the resurrection of the dead."[1] When he was among men he raised the dead.[2] He said: "The works that I do in my Father's name these bear witness of me."[3] "If I do not the works of my Father, believe me not. ... The Father is in me and I in the Father."[4] He claimed that he and God were one.[5] He alone knows and reveals God.[6]

"All authority", according to Matthew 28:18, belongs to him.

(1) *He possesses all legislative authority*. He alone has the right to make laws for the government of his people. "He is the Head of the body, the church." (Col. 1:18). An oracle from heaven said. "Hear him." (Matt. 17:5).

(2). *He possesses all judicial authority*. "The Father has given all judgment to the Son." (John 5:22). "He gave him authority to execute judgment." (John 5:27).

(3). *He possesses all executive authority*. "He is the King of kings, and Lord of lords." "He is the only Potentate." (I Tim. 6:15). "He must reign, till he has put all his enemies under his feet." (I Cor. 15:25). "He shall" at "the end" "deliver up the kingdom to God." (I Cor. 15:24). He is now a reigning as Prince in heaven. (Acts 5:31). Stephen saw him "standing on the right hand of God." (Acts 7:36).

---

[1] Romans 1:4
[2] Luke 7:11-16; Mark 5:22-24, 35-42; John 11:1-44
[3] John 10:24
[4] John 10:37-38
[5] John 10:30
[6] Matthew 11:27

Apart from Christ, ordinances have no value. Peter "commanded" Cornelius and his friends "to be baptized *in the name of* Jesus Christ."[1] Under the instruction of Paul, the twelve men whom he found in Ephesus, and who had not heard of the gift of the Holy Spirit, "were baptized *into the name of* the Lord Jesus."[2] In the communion the bread represents the body of Christ, and the fruit of the vine represents his blood.[3] The Lord's Supper is to be observed because the Christ said: "This do in remembrance of me."[4] In this service, disciples of Christ look back to his life on earth, and forward to his return from heaven. Baptism and the Supper of the Lord possess value because of their relation to, and their connection with, the Son of God.

All worship must be through the Lord Jesus. We are to "give thanks always for all things *in the name of* our Lord Jesus Christ to God;" and we are exhorted to subject ourselves to "one another in the fear of Christ."[5] "And whatsoever ye do, in word or in deed, *do all in the name of the Lord Jesus*,"[6] says Paul.

The Christ is "in the heavenly places, far above all rule, and authority, and power, and dominion, and every name that is named, not only in this world, but also in that which is to come; and" God "put all things in subjection under his feet, and gave him to be Head over all things."[7]

Exalting Christ thus in our thoughts, teaching, and lives, the people of Christ will be united, the Church will be made pure, and multitudes will turn to him, and share with us the joys of the great salvation.

REVIEW.
1.   Quote Alexander Proctor on Christ supreme.

---

[1] Acts 10:48
[2] Acts 19:1-5
[3] Matthew 26:26-28; Mark 14:22-24; Luke 22:14-20; 1 Corinthians 11:17-34
[4] 1 Corinthians 11:24
[5] Ephesians 5:20-21
[6] Colossians 3:17
[7] Ephesians 1:21-22

2. The divinity of Christ occupies what place in the teaching of the Disciples?
3. Why is Jesus called "the Son of God?"
4. To what did he appeal as evidence in support of his claims?
5. What three things are implied in the "All authority" attributed to Christ?
6. What value have the ordinances apart from him?
7. Through whom alone can acceptable worship be offered to God?
8. Where is the Christ now?
9. What will follow when we give Christ pre-eminence in all things?

Chapter Eleven

THE PLACE OF THE ORDINANCES

All evangelical Christians agree that the ordinances appointed by the Christ are two— baptism and the Supper of the Lord.

The Disciples teach that baptism is an immersion of penitent believers in water, in the name of the Christ and into the name of the Father, and of the Son, and of the Holy Spirit. No one denies that this is Christian baptism. This teaching and practice is therefore out of the region of controversy. Affusion—sprinkling and pouring—are in dispute. Many intelligent believers deny that affusion is baptism. The baptism of unbelievers—that is of infants—is in controversy. The baptism of such as believe on Christ and repent of their sins is not in debate. All agree that penitent believers are proper subjects for baptism. The teaching and practice of the Disciples on the subject of baptism— persons to be baptized and action—is out of the region of debate. They stand on unquestionably safe ground.

The Lord's Supper is a feast of love to be observed by those who have openly identified themselves with the Christ. The disciples of Jesus Christ alone were present when this ordinance was instituted.[1] Mem-

---

[1] Matthew 26:26-28

bers of the Church of God under the ministry of Apostles enjoyed the Lord's Supper.[1] The first Christians assembled on the first day of the week to break bread.[2] This ordinance is "a sweet and precious feast of holy memories, designed to quicken our love of Christ and cement the ties of our common brotherhood." "We, therefore, observe it as a part of our regular worship, every Lord's Day, and hold it a solemn, but joyful and refreshing feast of love, in which all disciples of our Lord should feel it to be a great privilege to unite." It is a "simple and solemn family feast in the Lord's house."

The place of baptism is after an experience of belief and penitence, and subsequent to a public confession of faith in the Son of God. The place of the Supper is in the church, and it was designed by the head of the body for such as, by faith and baptism, are members. The ordinances are, therefore, means of grace. Baptism is more than a mere form. It is an expression of faith and penitence. In this ordinance there is a public and formal recognition of the authority possessed by our Lord Jesus, and a surrendering to him. The language of the heart, in baptism, is: "Here, Lord, I give myself to thee." It is, therefore, more than simply a door into the church. Baptism brings the baptized "into Christ" and into a participation of the benefits purchased for us by the death of Christ. Hence we are said to be "baptized into his death."[3] Coming to baptism, with the spiritual preparation above indicated, one finds an assurance of acceptance with God—an assurance of salvation—which previously he did not possess.[4] What Mark in this place calls *salvation*, Luke and Peter call "remission of sins."[5]

The Disciples therefore teach the believing penitent to seek, through baptism, the divine assurance of the forgiveness of sins, and that gift

---

[1] 1 Corinthians 11:20-34, 1:2
[2] Acts 20:7
[3] Romans 6:3
[4] Mark 16:16
[5] Luke 24:47, Acts 2:38

of the Holy Spirit,[1] which the Lord has promised to them that obey him.[2]

> "Thus, in a hearty and scriptural surrender to the authority of the Lord Jesus, and not in dreams, visions, or revelations, are we to seek for that assurance of pardon and that evidence of sonship to which the gospel points us."

Baptism is said to "save us." (I Peter 3:21). But it cannot save without faith, since "without faith it is impossible to be well-pleasing" unto God. (Heb. 11:6). It does not save without penitence, since our Lord declared that the impenitent must perish. (Luke 13:3, 5). Nor does baptism save without the confession, since "with the mouth confession is made unto salvation," (Rom. 10:10). To be of any value the person baptized must call on the name of the Lord. So Ananias instructed Saul of Tarsus. (Acts 22:16) When Jesus "was baptized of John in the Jordan," (Mark 1:9,) he prayed. (Luke 3:21-22). It is impossible for baptism, or any other act of man, to merit salvation since according to the divine mercy men are saved. (Titus 3:5). Salvation is of grace. (Eph. 2:8). There is no power in water to cleanse from sin. Sin is a disease of the heart. Naaman was captain of the host of the King of Syria, and he was a great man, but he was a leper. The prophet Elisha told him to "go and wash in the Jordan seven times" and he would be made whole. He dipped seven times, "according to the saying of the man of God," and was cured of his disease. (II Kings 5:1, 10, 14). God cured him when he obeyed. There was no virtue in the Jordan water to remove leprosy. Jesus told the man who was born blind to "wash in the pool of Saloam." "He went away, therefore, and washed, and came seeing." (John 9:1-7). Neither the clay, with which Jesus anointed his eyes, nor the water in which he washed, gave sight to the blind man. The power of God did that; but this power was exercised when the man did what he was told to do. So there is nothing in baptism to mer-

---

[1] Acts 2:38
[2] Acts 5:32

it salvation, nor to take away sin, but God forgives, and gives an assurance of the fact when the sinner, in this ordinance, recognizes the authority of his Son and surrenders to him.

In the ordinances there is a symbolic setting forth of the great facts in the gospel. The Christ died for our sins, was buried, and rose again. (I Cor. 15:3-4). We die to sin, are buried in baptism, and rise to walk in newness of life. (Rom. 6:1-4). In the Lord's Supper there is a remembrance of the fact that we are sinners and that the Son of God died for us.

"This do in remembrance of me" said the Christ, at the institution of the Supper. (Luke 22:19). Paul says that "as often as ye eat this bread, and drink the cup, ye proclaim the Lord's death till he come." (I Cor. 11:26).

It is the peculiar glory of our religion that it is spiritual—spiritual in its origin, aim, methods, and results. The ordinances of Jesus Christ are to be used for our spiritual comfort and advancement. This is their place and use in the Christian system.

REVIEW.
1. The number and names of the ordinances.
2. In baptism, what practice is not in dispute?
3. What practices are in debate?
4. Describe the Lord's Supper.
5. Describe the place of baptism.
6. What is given to the penitent believer in baptism?
7. What text affirms that baptism saves?
8. What other things are essential to salvation?
9. How is the fact illustrated that there is no virtue in baptism?
10. What are set forth in the ordinances?

Chapter Twelve

MISUNDERSTANDING AND OPPOSITION

Jesus told his disciples that they would be hated by all men, and that the time would come when men would feel that they were rendering service to God by putting them to death. Saul of Tarsus had a conscience void of offence toward God when he bound and cast into prison men and women for no other reason than that they loved and obeyed Jesus. He thought he did right in doing this. The explanation, in part, is found in the fact that he did not understand Jesus nor his people. He said: "I did it ignorantly."[1] Many of the bitter contentions in the church have originated in ignorance. The ecclesiastical and theological warriors did not understand each other. This was true of much of the opposition encountered by Stone and the Campbells. Their aim was something of which the popular religious teachers had never heard. It seemed to them impossible to go back to the Christ and from him alone receive instruction as to what to believe and do in order to be saved. The plan was impractical. How one could be a Christian only, was apparently beyond their comprehension. The simple principle which was at the foundation of all that the reformers were attempting caused them to use language that their opponents did not under-

---

[1] 1 Timothy 1:12

stand. They had determined to reject the terminology of the schools—to speak of Bible things in Bible language. What does God say? In what language does he say it? That is what I will say; and the manner in which I will say it. This thought was fundamental in all that was undertaken by the great men who under God inaugurated this movement to return to the Christianity of the New Testament in doctrine, ordinance and life. Those who were not in sympathy and cooperation with them were apparently unable to comprehend a principle which to us, of the present day, is so exceedingly simple and obviously correct. They knew the language of the various schools of theology. They knew especially Calvinism and its language, but with the unadulterated Christianity of the Christ they were not acquainted, nor were they able to express their belief in the words of the Holy Spirit, in the New Testament. An honest misunderstanding led to bitter opposition. A movement inaugurated to bring about peace precipitated a season of violent contention.

But in attempting to understand this opposition to the efforts of holy men to improve the condition of a dismembered and comparatively impotent church, some account must be taken of the fact that the heart is deceitful and corrupt. There can be no reasonable doubt that some bad men—sectarian rather than Christian —were in the opposition. Their craft was in danger. If this movement succeeds our stipends will be taken from us. There were no doubt such men, but their number was comparatively small.

To illustrate the opposition of men whose intentions were good, but who did not understand the principle on which the new movement was based take the following:

1. The advocates of a return to primitive Christianity said not a word in their discourses about the doctrine of the Trinity. Why? There is nothing in the New Testament on the subject. It was, therefore, understood by the opponents that the divine nature of Jesus was denied. But instead of denying that the Son of Mary was God in human form, they affirmed it in the strongest possible language. Instead of derogat-

ing from the dignity and worth of our Savior they made a belief that he is THE Son of God an indispensable condition of baptism and church membership.

2. They did not employ language that was current in orthodox circles in speaking of the Holy Spirit and his work in regeneration and sanctification; nor did they pray that the Spirit might come in convicting and converting power; nor that men might receive the baptism of the Holy Ghost. It was thence inferred that the personality and work of the Holy Spirit in regeneration and sanctification were denied. The advocates of a purer teaching and practice believed that the Holy Spirit is a person, and that in regeneration and sanctification he employs the truth as his instrument.[1] They taught that the baptism of the Holy Spirit was administered on Pentecost, in Jerusalem, and at the house of Cornelius, in Caesarea, and is not for us.

3. And since persons who desired to be baptized were not asked to relate an experience, telling of wonderful things seen and heard, thought and felt, as was then the custom, the reformers were accused of denying "experimental religion." They did not, however, deny the existence, or importance, of what their opponents called "experimental religion." They could not approve of the language employed when speaking of experience, through which men pass in turning to God, nor could they endorse the use that was made of these experiences. Love, repentance, or such a sorrow for sin as issues in reformation, the faith that saves, ceasing to do evil, learning to do well are experiences. Religion is an intelligent conviction resulting in a return to the fellowship of God.

4. Because the advocates of the restoration of a pure faith and a pure speech spoke of baptism in the language of the New Testament, they were charged with believing in baptismal regeneration.[2] Their opponents, in their creeds and confessions of faith, were, however, more

---

[1] John 17:17; 1 Corinthians 12:3; James 1:18
[2] Mark 16:16; Acts 2:38; 22:16; 1 Peter 3:21; John 3:5

nearly committed to the doctrine. The reformers taught that "regeneration must be so far accomplished before baptism that the subject is changed in heart ... otherwise baptism is nothing but an empty form."

These days of misunderstanding and opposition are past. More and more, men of intelligence are coming to understand the principles, aims, and methods, of the Disciples of Christ and to enter into sympathy with them.

REVIEW.
1. Was the effort to unite Christians at first popular?
2. How do you account for the opposition?
3. What four illustrations are given to explain the misunderstanding and opposition?
4. What is now coming to pass?

Chapter Thirteen

RAPID INCREASE IN NUMBERS

Notwithstanding the gross misunderstanding, consequent misrepresentation, and determined opposition, the growth, in numbers, of the Disciples of Christ is one of the most wonderful facts in the history of American Christianity. From the first their progress was rapid, but their increase in numbers was never so great as at the present time. The Statistical Secretary reported to the General Convention in Indianapolis in October, 1897, that there are 10,029 churches, 1,051,079 members, 7,284 Sunday Schools, 676,949 pupils and teachers, and 5,780 preachers. Comparing this report with the one made in 1896, it is apparent that there was a gain during the year of 422 churches, 42,407 members, 627 Sunday Schools, 37,418 students and teachers, 420 ministers of the gospel. It is conceded by all persons who are in a position to know whereof they speak, that our numerical increase, by conversion, far exceeds that of any other people in the United States. How is this to be accounted for? What is the secret of this wonderful growth?

It is evident that in whatever way the fact here stated may be explained the Disciples have a message for the people. That they enlist the sympathy and cooperation of the people to so great an extent is a demonstration of this fact. The following are some of the reasons that may be assigned for our success in enlisting men in the service of Christ:

1. In the beginning of the movement the prevalent conception of Christianity was the Calvinistic. Calvinism contains five points as follows:

(1) Men are inherently and totally depraved.
(2) A definite number from all eternity were chosen of God unto eternal life without faith or works or any other thing on the part of man as a condition.
(3) Jesus died for the elect only. His atonement was limited. The benefits of his death were not for all men.
(4) Those who were elected and for whom Christ died are effectually called by the gospel.
(5) Such persons cannot fall away and be lost.

The preaching of the facts, truths, principles, precepts, promises, and warnings, of the gospel as contained in the New Testament, came to the people as a revelation from heaven. It antagonized Calvinism at every point. Many good people were on the verge of despair. They could not find an assurance of their election. They were not certain that Christ died for them. The new teaching assured them that Jesus tasted death for every man,[1] that the good news was to be preached to all,[2] and that the invitation to accept the purchased redemption was extended to all. "He that will, let him take the water of life freely."[3] This statement partially accounts for the rapid growth in numbers at first.

2. The plea for union is so reasonable, so scriptural, and so full of the spirit of the Prince of Peace, that it has from the beginning taken a strong hold on large numbers. It presented a marked contrast to the bitter strifes and sectarian contentions with which the church was cursed. Into the midst of this tumult the Disciples threw themselves saying: "Let us have peace." How? "By a return to the religion of Jesus

---

[1] Hebrews 2:9
[2] Matthew 28:18-20; Mark 16:15-16
[3] Revelation 22:17

as it is described in the New Testament—its faith, its ordinances, its life." The protest against the sin of division commended itself to good men, intelligent and fair-minded, as warranted by the word and Spirit of Holy Scripture. The prayer of the Savior is a sufficient warrant for the plea in behalf of unity and peace among those who believe.

3. The clear and Scriptural teaching as to the steps that men must take, according to the New Testament, to enjoy an assurance of salvation. They said: "He that hath ears, let him hear."[1] "Belief comes of hearing, and hearing by the Word of Christ."[2] "He that disbelieves shall be condemned."[3] "Without faith it is impossible to be well-pleasing" unto God.[4] "Believe on the Lord Jesus and thou shalt be saved."[5] God "commands men that they should all everywhere repent."[6] "Except ye repent, ye shall ... perish."[7] "With the mouth confession is made unto salvation."[8] "Who shall confess me before men, him will I also confess before my Father which is in heaven."[9] "Be baptized every one of you," who having heard now believe, repent and confess Christ, "unto the remission of your sins; and ye shall receive the gift of the Holy Spirit."[10] Baptism brings penitent believers into Christ.[11] Hence it is said to save.[12] This Scriptural, reasonable, logical and positive presentation of "the way of salvation," constantly supported by quotations and illustrations from the written Word, accounts in part for the success of the Disciples in gaining adherents.

---

[1] Matthew 13:43
[2] Romans 10:17
[3] Mark 16:16
[4] Hebrews 11:6
[5] Acts 16:31
[6] Acts 17:30
[7] Luke 13:3
[8] Romans 10:10
[9] Matthew 10:32
[10] Acts 2:38
[11] Romans 6:3
[12] 1 Peter 3:21

4. The encouragement that was, and is, given to all good men who have a sufficient knowledge of Scripture, without regard to the learning of the schools to "preach the Word" is an important item in the conditions leading to this success. There are no "clergymen" among the Disciples. "All ye are brethren," said the Master.[1] Some devote themselves entirely to teaching and preaching Christ, but they are still simply brethren —they are not "clergymen." All are encouraged to tell the good news publicly or privately. All are encouraged to do the work of missionaries. "He that heareth, let him say, Come."[2]

These are some of the reasons why the Disciples have increased in numbers so rapidly.

REVIEW.
1. How many churches?
2. How many members?
3. How many Sunday Schools?
4. How many teachers and pupils?
5. How many preachers?
6. What is evident from these facts?
7. What four reasons are given for the rapid growth of the Disciples?

---

[1] Matthew 23:8
[2] Revelation 22:17

Chapter Fourteen

DEEPENING SPIRITUAL LIFE

This movement for a return to New Testament Christianity is thoroughly spiritual. The period of misunderstanding and opposition obscured in a measure, this fact, but now that we are better understood and there is less opposition and contention the fact should be recalled. Among other things our fathers realized the inability of the popular conceptions of Christianity to produce the change of heart and life which the Scriptures make so essential to an entrance into the kingdom of glory. Mr. Campbell said in his debate with N.L. Rice, in Lexington, Kentucky, in 1843, that:

> "our reformation began in the conviction of the inadequacy of the corrupted forms of religion in popular use to effect that thorough change of heart and life which the gospel contemplates as so essential to admission into heaven." (Campbell and Rice Debate, p. 678).

They saw that the matter of supreme importance is character. What a man is—not what he owns, or says, or does—is of transcendent importance. God looks upon the heart. He knows men as they are. We know them as they seem to be. The purpose of the gospel is spirituality of character. The Holy Spirit working in the word and ordinances, under favorable circumstances produces one whose distinguishing peculiarities are "love, joy, peace, long-suffering, kindness, goodness, faithfulness, meekness, temperance" or self-control.[1] This character is called "the fruit of the Spirit" and "against such there is no law."

The mission of the Disciples is therefore largely to their brethren in the Protestant denominations. The members of these churches are openly on the side of Christ. They believe in and confess him. Their faces are turned toward the Sun of righteousness.[2] Their feet are in the way of righteousness. The Bible they receive as the Word of God. To them it is a precious word. These things they show to be true in many ways. Their lives as well as their words testify to them. But there are some things in the way of the largest attainments in the spiritual life. There are errors in doctrines. Some dogmas are believed for which there is no warrant in Scripture. For some of their practices there cannot be produced a "thus saith the Lord" either "in expressed terms or approved precedent." Human creeds and names never applied by the Holy Spirit to the children of God in the New Testament encourage a party spirit. Such a spirit is diametrically opposed to the spirit of the Christ. The ordinances are frequently misplaced. The spiritual profit that ought, therefore, to be derived from them is not realized. The Bible can be more intelligently used. When more rationally read there will be realized a greater helpfulness and joy. It is the work of the Disciples of Christ to cultivate, in their associations with these people, a fraternal spirit, and to help them into lives more like the simple, sweet, spiritual life of the Son of Man.

But to do this they must nurture in themselves, and seek to deepen and broaden, the life that "is hid with Christ in God."[3] Example is more potent than speech. What we are is more eloquent than what we say. When words and deeds are alike spiritual there is great power over men for good. There are three conditions for health. These conditions are as essential to spiritual as to bodily health.

---

[1] Galatians 5:22
[2] Malachi 4:2
[3] Colossians 3:3

1. Pure Air. Good health cannot be enjoyed in a vitiated atmosphere. This is true of the body. It is equally true of the spirit. There is a spiritual atmosphere as there is a material. The one no less certainly than the other may be foul. Disciples, therefore, if they would experience a deep, pure, vigorous, spiritual life must be careful to abide, as far as possible, in a wholesome spiritual atmosphere. This is found in the Christian home, in the assembled church, in the Sunday School, and other similar conventions. Men and women who walk with Christ are spiritually helpful. Seek their companionship. Be much in the company with those who are much in company with the Christ. "Evil company doth corrupt good manners."[1] Good company has a tendency to purify bad manners. We breathe a pure atmosphere when in the society of good men and women.

2. Wholesome Food. The Word of God is soul food. Simon Peter said: "As newborn babes, long for the spiritual milk which is without guile, that ye may grow thereby unto salvation; if ye have tasted that the Lord is gracious."[2] "All wickedness and all guile, and hypocrisies, and envies, and all evil speakings" are to be put away. Those who feed regularly on the Word will grow strong. Faith is produced and nourished by the Word.[3] The goodness of God leads to repentance,[4] but this is revealed to men in the Word that he inspired. "We love, because he first loved us,"[5] but the fact that God commends his love toward us in that while we were yet sinners Christ died for us,[6] is recorded in Holy Scripture. Reading, therefore, these sacred writings and giving heed to their exposition, meantime meditating thereupon, will deepen and broaden the current of the spiritual life. This food ought to be taken regularly. The Bereans searched the Scriptures daily.[7] To

---

[1] 1 Corinthians 15:33
[2] 1 Peter 2:2
[3] Romans 10:17; John 20:30-31
[4] Romans 2:4
[5] 1 John 4:19
[6] Romans 5:8
[7] Acts 17:11

the souls of saints the Word of the Lord is very precious. Read Psalm 119.

3. Exercise. One may have pure air and wholesome food, but without exercise there will not be vigorous health. Christians ought to exercise themselves in the observance of the ordinances, the regular acts of devotion, in private and in the assembly of God's people, and in doing good. Our eternal destiny depends on this.[1] Our present spiritual health depends on the service that we render to God and to men for his sake.

From first to last the plea of the Disciples is for a deeper spiritual life. The unity of God's people for which they plead is thoroughly spiritual. As the Father and Son are one, so ought believers to be one.[2] But this is intensely spiritual. The same statement may be made, with equal truth, concerning every item in their teaching and practice.

REVIEW.
1. What is the marked peculiarity of the plea of the Disciples?
2. Their mission is therefore to whom?
3. What then should be our bearing toward other Christians?
4. What kind of culture is now especially needed?
5. What are three conditions of health?
6. Where is a wholesome spiritual atmosphere?
7. What is the soul's food?
8. What character of exercise will promote spiritual health?
9. What is the nature of the union for which the Disciples plead?

---

[1] Matthew 25:31-46
[2] John 17:20-21

Chapter Fifteen

EVANGELISTIC SPIRIT AMONG THE DISCIPLES

1. The Disciples are both evangelical and evangelistic. Their teaching and practice are in harmony with the gospel. This makes them evangelical. They present the good news for the purpose of winning men to Christ and in such a manner as to enlist men in his service. This makes them evangelistic. Their evangelism is one of the marked features of their history. The fundamental position which they assumed at the first, and to which they now steadfastly adhere, compels them to be evangelical and evangelistic. This position is that every item of faith and conduct must have a warrant in the Word of God. This word is the supreme and sole authority in the religious belief and life. "Where the Scriptures speak we will speak, and where the Scriptures are silent we are silent."

2. Man is a sinner. He is dead in sins. His iniquities separate him from God. The depravity of man is universal. All sin and fall short of the glory of God. His ruin is complete. Without Divine interposition deliverance is impossible. Man cannot save himself. Law cannot save him. Salvation is of grace. The problem of the ages is as to how man can be justified in the sight of God. Apart from the revelation of God in Christ the problem is insoluble. The grace of God made known in Christ contains the solution. These things concerning the lost and helpless estate

of man are taught in both Testaments. And this teaching is at the foundation of all evangelistic and missionary effort. If man is not lost why did Christ die? The agony of the Son of Man in the garden and on the cross testifies as nothing else can to the utter ruin of man.

3. But the creature has power to choose and to refuse his Creator. It is a terrible power, but it belongs to man. He can believe, he can love, he can obey. He also has power to disbelieve, to hate, to disobey. Hence the invitations, arguments, appeals, of the gospel. "Come and let us reason together saith the Lord."[1] "Come unto me ... and I will give you rest."[2] "Though your sins be as scarlet, they shall be as white as snow; though they be red like crimson, they shall be as wool," etc.[3] "Ye will not come to me, that ye may have life."[4] "He that will, let him take the water of life freely."[5] There is no fatalism in the Bible. There is no unconditional election and reprobation in the joyful message. People entertaining these thoughts must be evangelistic. Such beliefs gender and nurture the spirit of evangelism.

4. The Scriptures clearly teach that the gospel of the Christ is the power of God to save all who believe.[6] Hence the gospel was preached, and only this, by the Apostles of Christ. Paul was determined to know only the crucified Christ in his sacred ministry.[7] He regarded the Christ suffering for our sins as the power and wisdom of God.[8] To philosophers this message seemed foolishness; to self-reliant and self-satisfied men it seemed to be only weakness, but "the foolishness of God is wiser than men; and the weakness of God is stronger than men."[9] By the faithful preaching of Christ crucified foul men were

---

[1] Isaiah 1:18
[2] Matthew 11:28
[3] Isaiah 1:18-20
[4] John 5:40
[5] Revelation 22:17
[6] Romans 11:6; 1 Corinthians 15:1-2
[7] 1 Corinthians 2:2
[8] 1 Corinthians 1:24
[9] 1 Corinthians 1:25

made clean and bad men good, in Corinth,[1] and the same message preached with a similar zeal and in the same spirit at the present time will produce equally encouraging results. This is the belief of the Disciples of Christ; hence their evangelistic spirit.

5. Man is intelligent and free. He can both reason and choose. The Scriptures assume that conviction and choice result from intelligence. Hence the holy men sent by the Christ to evangelize the people, in their preaching, reasoned with those whom they met. Wicked men "were not able to withstand the wisdom and the spirit by which" Stephen "spoke."[2] Philip, the evangelist, so reasoned with the treasurer of Queen Candace, out of the Scriptures, that he became a Christian.[3] Three weeks were spent by Paul reasoning with the Jews in their synagogue in Thessalonica.[4] "Some of them were persuaded, and consorted with Paul and Silas; and of the devout Greeks a great multitude, and of the chief women not a few."[5] Paul and Barnabas "so spake" in "the synagogue of the Jews. ...in Iconium ...that a great multitude both of the Jews and of the Greeks believed."[6] Belief in Jesus as the Son of God and our Savior comes as a result of hearing the word of Christ. The preached word produces faith.[7] Upon this fact the Disciples place much emphasis. Hence their evangelistic spirit.

6. In all times, places, and things, the Christ must have the preeminence. He is Lord.[8] He alone is to be heard.[9] He has superseded Moses and the prophets. All authority now belongs to him.[10] To diso-

---

[1] 1 Corinthians 6:9-11
[2] Acts 6:10
[3] Acts 8:26-40
[4] Acts 17:2
[5] Acts 17:4
[6] Acts 14:1
[7] Romans 10:13-17
[8] Acts 2:36, 10:36
[9] Matthew 17:5
[10] Matthew 28:18

bey him is to fail of salvation.[1] But his command is to "make disciples of all the nations."[2] He requires his disciples to "preach the gospel to the whole creation."[3] To neglect, or to refuse to preach the gospel in obedience to our Lord's command is to be guilty of disobedience. This we believe and teach. Hence the evangelistic spirit among the Disciples of Christ.

But this work they cannot do in their own strength. This our Lord knew. He therefore said: "I am with you always."[4] In this fact there is encouragement to undertake the work. The presence and approval of the Christ accounts for their success in turning men from Satan to God.

REVIEW.
1. What is here claimed for the Disciples?
2. What is it to be evangelical?
3. What to be evangelistic?
4. How can one account for the evangelistic spirit among Disciples?
5. In whose strength can we succeed in evangelizing the world?

------

[1] Hebrews 5:9
[2] Matthew 28:19
[3] Mark 16:15
[4] Matthew 28:20

Chapter Sixteen

THE LITERATURE OF THE DISCIPLES

The first literature of the Disciples was polemic in character. This was occasioned by circumstances. They were misunderstood. False accusations were made concerning their teaching. Their pacific desires were misrepresented because they were not understood. Controversy became, in this way, for a time, a feature of their life. Thus it came to pass that their early literature was in this tone.

The first periodical published in the interest of union, by a restoration of the doctrine, ordinances, and life, of the apostolic age was called the *Christian Baptist*. Alexander Campbell was both editor and proprietor. The place of publication was Bethany, Brooke Co., Virginia, now West Virginia. The paper was issued once a month. The first number was dated August 1, 1823. Its general character and object were stated in the following words:

> *The Christian Baptist* shall espouse the cause of no religious sect, excepting that ancient sect 'called Christians first at Antioch.' Its sole object shall be the eviction of truth and the exposing of error in doctrine and practice. The editor, acknowledging no standard of religious faith or works other than the Old and New Testaments, and

the latter as the only standard of the religion of Jesus Christ, will, intentionally at least, oppose nothing which it contains and recommend nothing which it does not enjoin. Having no worldly interest at stake from the adoption or reprobation of any articles of faith or religious practice, having no gift nor religious emolument to blind his eyes or to pervert his judgment, he hopes to manifest that he is an impartial advocate of truth.

The *Christian Baptist* continued seven years. Its style was caustic, cutting, severe. The editor adopted this manner to gain the attention of the people, to awaken them to a sense of the condition of the church, and to excite in their minds a desire for something better. *The Millennial Harbinger* followed the *Christian Baptist*. Its tone was milder— more pacific. The purpose of the *Christian Baptist* had been attained.

The Disciples have published two translations of the New Testament. The first was the work of Alexander Campbell in 1826, and the second was by H.T. Anderson in 1864. The title of Mr. Campbell's work was, "The Living Oracles." "The Christian System" is a non-controversial book, written by Alexander Campbell, which very fully sets forth his understanding of the faith and practice authorized by the New Testament.

J.T. Barclay spent some years, as a missionary, in Jerusalem, and as a result wrote a book of unusual merit entitled "The City of the Great King." Subsequent writers on the Holy Land have drawn freely upon Dr. Barclay's work.

Two volumes by Robert Milligan entitled "Reason and Revelation," and "The Scheme of Redemption," are intended to exhibit, in a formal and somewhat elaborate way, reasons for believing in the Bible as a supernatural book, and in Jesus as the Son of God; and to place before the mind of the reader the divine plan of redemption as outlined in the Word of God.

"The Divine Demonstration," is a book on the truth of the Christian religion, by H.W. Everest.

J.S. Lamar is the author of a book entitled "First Principles and Perfection." In this work he shows how persons become Christians and how they can grow in grace.

"McGarvey's Commentary on Acts," is a good book on conversion, or how men became Christians under the ministry of specially inspired men. He is also the author of "The Text and the Canon;" a work to be read by those who desire to have clear views as to the origin, and structure of the New Testament; and reasons for believing that its writings are inspired. President McGarvey's, "The Land and the Book," is an excellent work on Palestine. The Holy Land and the Holy Book are shown to sustain such relations to each other that the reading of the volume, here named, will strengthen one's faith in the "Old Book."

In "Jesus as a Teacher," by B.A. Hinsdale, the second part, the origin and growth of the New Testament is shown.

"The Old Faith Restated," is a volume written by a number of Disciples, and edited by J. H. Garrison. As the name suggests it contains a statement of the teaching of reason and revelation on a variety of topics of current interest connected with the faith once for all delivered to the saints.

F.M. Green's "History of Missions Among the Disciples" is the only book of its kind in existence. It was written a number of years ago and is chiefly valuable as containing an account of the origin of organized mission work among the Disciples.

A. McLean's "Missionary Addresses" is a book worthy of place in any library. The author's intense and intelligent enthusiasm for missions is realized on every page.

For an intelligent understanding of the origin and history of the Disciples there are two books that must be read: "Memoirs of A. Camp-

bell," by Robert Richardson; and "The Life of Isaac Errett," by J.S Lamar.

There is space to mention the following books, devotional in character: "The Heavenly Way," and "Alone with God," by J.H. Garrison;
"Walks About Jerusalem," "Letters to a Young Christian," and "Eve-
nings With the Bible," by Isaac Errett.

REVIEW.
1. Character of the first literature and reasons for?
2. The first periodical?
    a. When?
    b. Where?
    c. By whom edited?
    d. Its characteristics and reasons for?
3. New Testament translations?
    a. By whom?
    b. When published?
4. Name books setting forth the teaching of the New Testament.
5. Books on conversion or how to become Christians.
6. Works on missions.
7. Books on the truth of the Christian religion.
8. Books on the origin and structure of the New Testament.
9. Essential books to know the history of the Disciples?
10. Name devotional books.
11. Name the writers of all the books mentioned in this chapter.

Chapter Seventeen

EDUCATION AMONG THE DISCIPLES

The prime movers in the current effort to unite the people of God for world-wide evangelistic effort by a restoration of simple New Testament Christianity were educated men. As a result they had proceeded but a short distance in their attempt to return to primitive Christianity when the subject of education enlisted their attention and interest.

The first institution of higher education established by the Disciples was Bacon College, which was founded in Georgetown, Ky., in 1836. After a varied history it became Kentucky University in Lexington, Ky., in 1858.

Alexander Campbell, in 1838, published the plan of an institution of learning differing in important features from any college in existence. The teaching was to be essentially and permanently Biblical. All science, literature and art, were to be made tributary to the Bible. Moral character was to be an essential part of education. Mr. Campbell was especially impressed with the great need of an educated and efficient ministry to cooperate in the great work of restoring to the world the Christianity of Christ in its doctrine and life. As a result of his efforts Bethany College was granted a charter by the Legislature of Virginia in 1840. This work Mr. Campbell regarded as the consummation and crown of all his earthly projects. The Bible is a text book in this institution. The religious life of the college has been conspicuous from the first. No person received a diploma during Alexander Campbell's presidency, which was from the founding of the school until his death in 1866, who had not stood an examination in the Bible. In 1891 ninety-four percent of the students were Christians.

Eureka College, located in the town of Eureka, Ill., was chartered in 1855. The distinguishing feature of Bethany, as to the Bible, was reproduced in Eureka College. But from the first both sexes were admitted to Eureka College classes on terms of perfect equality. In the beginning this was not a custom in Bethany College, although for a number of years ladies have been admitted to its class rooms on the same terms as young men.

The North Western Christian University, now Butler University, Irvington, Ind., near Indianapolis, probably was the first college in the world to disregard sex distinctions in the Curriculum, Eureka College located at Eureka, Ill., was the next.

Hiram College, in a village of this name, twenty miles from Cleveland, Ohio, began in 1850 as the Western Reserve Eclectic Institute. It became Hiram College in 1867. The aims of the Eclectic Institute were:

> (1) "To provide a sound scientific and literary education.
> (2) To temper and sweeten such education with moral scriptural knowledge, and
> (3) To educate young men for the ministry."

James A. Garfield, twentieth President of the United States, was educated at the Western Reserve Eclectic Institute, and was a Professor in Hiram College.

Eminence College, located at Eminence, Henry County, Ky., was established in 1857. It is a personal enterprise inaugurated and carried forward by W.S. Giltner, but in the interests of the Disciples of Christ.

The Legislature of Iowa granted a charter to Oskaloosa College in 1857. This institution is the result of an organized effort on the part of the Disciples of Christ in Iowa, and is located in the town of Oskaloosa. In 1855 the Disciples in convention, in that State, resolved to establish a college.

Drake University, located at Des Moines, Iowa, was founded in 1881 by General F.M. Drake.

There is not space to give a list of all the colleges founded and conducted by the Disciples of Christ, nor is it necessary to do so. The institutions here named are the most prominent and serve to show the interest which the Disciples feel in the cause of education. By their principles and aims the Disciples must be keenly alive to the cause of education.

The General Convention has a Board of Education, the purpose of which will be found in the nineteenth chapter of this book. It has in hand a movement to employ a competent person to visit our colleges and deliver lectures on missions and mission work.

The Christian Woman's Board of Missions three or four years ago established two chairs in connection with the University of Michigan, the purpose of which is to give instruction in the English Bible. The work is so practical and popular that the Disciples are doing a similar work in connection with five other State Universities.

REVIEW.

1. What kind of men, as to learning, were the prime movers in the attempt to restore New Testament Christianity?
2. When and where was the first college organized?
3. At what time did Alexander Campbell publish the plan of an institution of learning?
    a. What was to be its peculiarity?
    b. Result?
4. What other colleges are named?
    a. Date and beginning of each?

    b. Where located?
5. Name the first college in the world to admit women to its classes?
6. The Board of Education, its purpose, and the special work now in hand?
7. Work of Bible instruction in connection with State Universities?

Chapter Eighteen

CHRISTIAN ENDEAVOR AMONG THE DISCIPLES

With the spirit and aim of the Disciples before us it ought to occasion no surprise that when the Christian Endeavor movement came into existence they gave to it a cordial welcome. "The Active Member's Pledge" is a good statement of what the Disciples aim to be and to do.

> "Trusting in the Lord Jesus Christ for strength, I promise him that I will strive to do whatever he would like to have me do; that I will make it the rule of my life to pray and to read the Bible every day, and to support my own church in every way, especially by attending all her regular Sunday and midweek services, unless prevented by some reason which I can conscientiously give to my Savior; and that, just so far as I know how, throughout my whole life, I will endeavor to lead a Christian life."

The Christ is given the pre-eminence. He is recognized as the Lord. The covenant is made with him. The promise is to read the Word of which he is the Alpha and Omega. The pledge is to strive to please him. His church is to be supported. The only reason for absence from a regular meeting of the church must be such as one can render to him. The life that is to be led is a simple Christian life. The Christ is to be in all things the model. What would he do if he were in my place? The reply to this question is the solution of all practical questions. The Endeavorer says, in a word, that "trusting in the Lord Jesus Christ for strength," he will endeavor to be and do all that the Lord Jesus would like to have him to be and to do. All of this, essential to the Christian Endeavor movement, is in perfect accord with the fundamental principles and aims of the Disciples of Christ,

The annual report of the National Superintendent of Christian Endeavor, made to the General Convention of Disciples of Christ, in Springfield Ill., in October, 1896, contained the following:

> "The religious training of our young people stands second to no interest among us. If the churches of tomorrow are to be intelligently aggressive and thoroughly loyal to our Lord; if they are to be well-equipped for effective service at home and abroad, we must thoroughly instruct and wisely train the young people of today."

> "The Christian Endeavor Societies offer to us the means through which these ends may be attained. These societies are simply groups of young Christians banded together by a definite pledge of loyalty to our Lord, for their training in his service. These societies are subordinate to the local churches in which they exist, and the normal development of their activities is through the channels of the churches. The permanent motto of the Christian Endeavor movement is 'For Christ and the Church.' It is not for itself."

In his report to the General Convention in 1897 the National Superintendent said:

> "Three years ago, at Richmond, I reported 2,446 societies; two years ago, at Dallas, I reported 3,085; one year

ago, at Springfield, I reported 3,654; today I report 3,987, a net gain of 333 societies."

Secretary Baer, in his annual report to the International Christian Endeavor Convention in San Francisco, in July, 1897, said that the Disciples of Christ stand third in the number of societies. The order is as follows: Presbyterians, Congregationalists, Disciples of Christ.

At the International Christian Endeavor Convention in Washington City, July, 1896, the Disciples in their rally appointed a committee on "Literature Among Our Young People." This committee reported to the Springfield Convention recommending "helps for the systematic reading of the Bible, a selected course of reading concerning missions in general, and our own missions in particular, and thorough instruction as to the origin, the principles, and the history of our own movement for the restoration of New Testament Christianity." This report was unanimously adopted by the convention and thus was originated the Bethany C. E. Reading Courses.

The first Lord's Day in February is observed as Christian Endeavor Day, and the object is to foster an interest in Foreign Missions. This convention also recommended "in addition, the establishment of Forefather's Day on the Lord's day nearest the 12th of October." It was farther "recommended that the purpose of this day be the fostering of interest in the study of the history and purpose of our people and, therefore, in our Home Missionary Work." Offerings may be made on these days of money, to aid the interests to which especial attention is called by their observance.

The Disciples of Christ extend a welcome to Christian Endeavor beyond that of any other people. Their organization in the interest of this uprising of the young people "For Christ and the Church" consists of local societies, local unions, state superintendents, a national superintendent, and two representatives on the Board of Trustees of the United Society. The pastors and elders in our churches are ex-officio members of the local societies and of the executive committee in each society.

The Christian Endeavorers among us have erected a chapel at Salt Lake City, in Utah. They assist our mission work in Boston and Chicago, and contribute to the treasuries of all the missionary organizations of the Disciples of Christ. Their work steadily increases in efficiency. There is in it the promise that the Church of the future will be better, more intelligent and consecrated to the Christ and his service than is the Church of today.

REVIEW.

1. Explain why Disciples cordially favor Christian Endeavor.
2. Give Endeavor statistics among Disciples of Christ.
3. What suggestion was made by the National Superintendent to the General Convention of Disciples in 1896?
4. What action was taken in Washington City, July, 1896 and its result?
5. Christian Endeavor Day and its object?
6. Forefather's Day and its purpose?
7. What is our general organization of Christian Endeavor?
8. What have Endeavorers done, among Disciples, in mission work?

Chapter Nineteen

MISSION WORK OF

THE DISCIPLES

It inevitable that with their conception of man in his fallen estate, of sin and its dire results, and of the Gospel as the divinely ordained remedy, the Disciples should, at an early period in their history, organize for mission work. The following is a condensed statement of facts concerning their organized efforts to preach the Gospel to all men:

The American Christian Missionary Society was organized in Cincinnati in 1849. The purpose of this Society was to give the Word of life to the people of our own and other lands. At present it is the National Home Mission Society of the Disciples of Christ. At the time of its organization Alexander Campbell was elected president, in which office he remained until his death in 1866.[1]

Since 1849 the American Christian Missionary Society has received $718,137.26; and 31,204 persons have been added to the churches, by confession and baptism, under the labors of its evangelists. Forty-six persons were in its service during the whole or a portion of the year ending October 1st, 1897. The number of baptisms was 3,174. The

---

[1] Alexander Campbell, who was not present at the meeting, was elected "president for life" without his knowledge or authorization.

amount of money collected was $44,365. Each dollar collected for missions secures the collection and expenditure of three dollars more, so that this society has been the means of securing more than two million dollars for Christian work, besides the money that has passed through its treasury. The work of this organization is chiefly in the states and territories of the West, and in the Atlantic and Gulf states. It is composed of life directors, life members, annual members, and delegates of churches. The office of the American Christian Missionary Society is in Cincinnati. Benj. L. Smith is the corresponding secretary.

In connection with this society are the Board of Church Extension, the Board of Negro Education and Evangelization, the Board of Education and the Board of Ministerial Relief.

The Board of Church Extension was organized in Cincinnati in 1883. In 1888 its office was removed to Kansas City, Mo. The object of this board is to aid homeless bands of Disciples to obtain houses of worship, by loaning them money at the low rate of four percent interest per year for five years. This fund has been handled with such wisdom that not a dollar has been lost. It now (January 30th, 1898) has on hand $152,000. Three hundred and seventy churches in thirty-six states and territories have been aided. G.W. Muckley, Kansas City, Mo., is the corresponding secretary.

The American Christian Missionary Society carries on educational and evangelistic work among the negroes in the South. The Southern Christian Institute is located at Edwards, Miss. J.B. Lehman is president. About one hundred pupils are enrolled annually. A.J. Thompson is president of the Louisville Bible School. The average annual attendance is twenty-four. Young men of color are here trained to be preachers of the gospel among their own people. Robert Brooks, the principal of the Mount Willing School, was educated in the Southern Christian Institute. Eighty-five pupils were enrolled during the last school year. The work of evangelization among the people of color in Missouri, Mississippi and Florida, has also received assistance during this time. A plantation of 800 acres belongs to the Southern Christian Institute.

Collections for the above named organizations, except the Boards of Ministerial Relief and Education, are taken as follows: By the churches, for general evangelization, the first Lord's Day in May; and by the Sunday Schools, for the same purpose, the first Lord's Day in December. For the Church Extension Fund the first Lord's Day in September.

The Board of Education was organized in 1894 in Richmond, Va. Its aim is to collect and publish statistics of education among the Disciples of Christ and foster their educational interests. Mrs. Albertina Allen Forest, Irvington, Ind., is the secretary.

The Board of Ministerial Relief was organized in Dallas, Texas, in 1895. A.M. Atkinson, Wabash, Ind., is the corresponding secretary. This board cares for aged and disabled ministers and their families. No one day in the year has been set apart for a collection in support of this ministry of love. Every Lord's Day is sacred to it. "Ye have the poor always with you."

The Christian Woman's Board of Missions was organized in Cincinnati in 1874. This society has the honor of being the first organization in the world for mission work in which the entire management is in the hands of women. The aggregate amount of money received is more than $600,000. It publishes two papers monthly: The Missionary Tidings, and The Junior Builders. Leaflets containing missionary intelligence, and appeals, are also published. Societies auxiliary to The Christian Woman's Board of Missions exist in thirty-five states and territories with a membership of 30,367. Among the young people there are Mission Bands and Circles, and Junior Endeavor Societies, in thirty-five states, with a membership of 16,938. Two persons are at work, under the auspices of this society, in Mexico; five in Jamaica, seventeen in India; and twenty-four in the United States. Miss Lois A. White, Indianapolis, Ind., is the corresponding secretary. Collections in the churches, the first Lord's Day in July.

The Foreign Christian Missionary Society was organized in Louisville, Ky., 1875. The aim of this society is to "make disciples of all the nations." One hundred and sixty-two persons are in its employ, working in England, Scandinavia, Turkey, India, China, Japan and Africa. The total receipts from its organization to October 1, 1897, were $1,008,943.61. The receipts from October 1, 1896, to the corresponding date in 1897, were $106,222.10. This amount was contributed by 2,586 churches, 2,810 Sunday Schools, 528 Societies of Christian Endeavor. A. McLean, Cincinnati, Ohio, is corresponding secretary.

There are also organizations, in the states and territories, in which there are Disciples, and in the District of Columbia, for home mission work.

REVIEW.
1. What are the names of the various missionary organizations?
2. Mention the field occupied by each.
3. Name the Secretaries and give their addresses.
4. Give the dates of organization of each of the Societies and Boards.
5. On what days are collections taken?
6. Name the Boards for which no days are specified.
7. Give the amount of money collected by each Society and Board.
8. Besides the Societies and Boards named in this chapter, what other missionary organizations are there?

Chapter Twenty

THE PRESENT STATE

OF THE UNION QUESTION

Since the publication of Thomas Campbell's "Declaration and Address" in 1809, a great change has taken place on the subject of union among those who believe in Jesus to the saving of the soul. It was necessary, at that time, to show by the Scriptures that such divisions as existed among Christians, and now exist, are sinful. The present divided condition of the church is not well-pleasing to the head of the body. This proposition was stoutly and generally denied then; not so at the present time. Divisions among the disciples of the peerless teacher are now lamented. Sectarianism is now condemned. The best men in the ministry now confess that sects are sinful. They are products of the flesh, not of the Holy Spirit. Good men pray and plead for Christian unity and union. Temporary unions are formed for evangelistic and other Christian purposes. There is a general agreement that there must be, for the children of God, a more excellent way than that in which we are walking at the present time. The one great point that has been gained since the agitation of this subject began in the early part of the present century is this: Schisms are sinful. The problem now is as to the character, the extent and Scriptural basis of union. The union for which Jesus prayed and which alone will be acceptable to him is spiritual in its character. It must be a union similar to that which exists between the Father and the Son.[1] This was the kind of unity which existed at the first among believers.[2] Paul says that believers ought to be perfectly joined together in the same mind and in the same judgment, and that they ought to speak the same things.[3] A number of bases for the union of Christians are now before the world.

I. There is the plan that may be fittingly characterized by the word *Submission*. The Pope laments the divided state of Christendom. He earnestly desires union. His plan is exceedingly simple. Let the heretical Protestant sects return to "the holy mother church," the Roman Catholic; let them acknowledge the Pope as the vicegerent of the crowned Christ, and humbly submit to him (the Pope), as to God. This is the plan of "his holiness," Leo XIII.

II. The word *Consolidation* describes another plan. It is that of the House of Bishops of the Protestant Episcopal Church, This plan proposes the reunion of the church on the following basis:

1) "The Holy Scriptures of the Old and New Testaments as 'containing all things necessary to salvation,' and as being the rule and ultimate standard of faith.
2) "The Apostles' Creed as being the baptismal symbol, and the Nicene Creed as the sufficient statement of the Christian faith.
3) "The two Sacraments ordained by Christ himself—baptism and the Supper of the Lord—ministered with unfailing use of Christ's words of institution, and of the elements ordained by him.
4) "The Historic Episcopate, locally adapted in the methods of its administration to the varying needs of the nations and peoples called of God into the unity of his Church."

---

[1] John 17:20-21
[2] Acts 4:32-35
[3] 1 Corinthians 1:10

This proposition, since its publication in 1886, has been widely discussed. "The Historic Episcopate locally adapted," etc., has excited the greatest interest. But the above plan contemplates Church union rather than Christian union.

III. *Confederation*, or *Federation*, is the word to use in describing another basis of union. This plan meets with most favor among Presbyterians. The late James McCosh, of Princeton University, was an earnest and able advocate of this scheme. Some of the smaller Presbyterian bodies have entered into a federation for Christian effort. In some of the cities this plan is being tried. Congregations of different denominations have gone into it. It proposes to leave denominational organizations and institutions as they are. Work common to all will be done by united effort. The relation of the several denominations to the federation, if the plan should be carried out, would be similar to that of the states of our Republic to the general government.

IV. A basis of union submitted by the Congregationalists may be described by the word *Compromise*. The Scriptures of the old and New Testament are to be recognized as containing God's word to man. As to the organization and order of the church and concerning the use, or non-use of baptism and the Lord's Supper, this plan says, in effect: "Let every man be persuaded in his own mind. If he desires to be immersed, or to immerse, so be it. If he prefers sprinkling or pouring let no one say nay. Or if, like the Quaker, he rejects both baptism and the Supper of the Lord, let him still be received and treated as a brother beloved."

V. *Restoration* is the word that describes the way to union advocated by the Disciples of Christ. "Back to Christ," is their watchword. "Hear ye him," is the oracle from heaven.[1] Paul affirms that the Christ is the only foundation for the church.[2] When he said this he was discussing the question of union among Christians. To believe in Christ and obey

---

[1] Matthew 17:5
[2] 1 Corinthians 3:11

him is the way to union. This plan has been presented at sufficient length in the preceding chapters. There is no better summary statement of this plan for our day than this: (1) The Primitive Creed, (2) The Primitive Ordinances, (3) The Primitive life.

REVIEW.
1. What change has taken place since 1809?
2. What are now the questions concerning the union?
3. What, at present, is the chief question?
4. How many bases of union are now before the public?
    a. Name and explain each.
    b. Which one do you prefer?
    c. Why?
5. Will there ever be a more perfect union among believers than at present exists?
    a. Why do you so think?

Chapter Twenty-One

POINTS TO BE GUARDED

Dr. Arthur T. Pierson says:

> It is remarkable, as a historic fact, that, just so soon as any movement, though beginning with a spiritual impulse and even in the spirit of protest and reform, gets to be popular and numerically strong, its point of peril is reached, if, indeed, it be not already disastrously passed; and the way that was once costly to enter and hard to follow, now becomes easy to enter and correspondingly pleasant to pursue. It is one of the paradoxes of history that the church, born in persecution and baptized in blood, no sooner grows to be numerous and strong than it begins to broaden out its doctrinal beliefs and to compromise with the secular spirit of the age; and there is more than one case in history where the same body of believers that once led the way in protest against heresy, afterward led the way in countenancing heresy; so that those who once separated from others for the sake of holy living, need to be separated from, by those who would live holy. (The Acts of the Holy Spirit, pp, 39-40).

The events that have taken place in the world, more especially in the church, ought to warn us against the perils to which we are exposed. Every great movement, every good thing, has its dangers. To this statement of fact the Disciples of Christ are not an exception. They are exposed to perils. What are some of the danger points in their experience?

Attention has been called to their rapid numerical increase. They are now, comparatively, popular. With their increase in numbers there has come, as is but natural, an increase of wealth. The possession of wealth is perilous. A church possessing much of this world's goods is in danger of saying, as did the church of Laodicea: "I am rich, and have gotten riches, and have need of nothing." Wealth is good if it is sanctified. But there is danger that with large possessions there will come to be luxurious habits of life. Effeminacy belongs to this manner of living. There is danger also of selfishness. These things are contrary to the Christian spirit. Especially guard the points here indicated. They are real perils to the work to which the Disciples of Christ have been called.

The inauguration of the movement, of which a brief account is given in these pages, was of God. He has cared for it from the first. It is manifestly a child of Divine Providence. To him we are indebted for whatever of success has attended our efforts. "Not by might nor by power, but by my Spirit, saith the Lord of Hosts."[1] Paul may plant, Apollos may water, but God gives the increase.[2] Of this fact we need to be frequently reminded. There is danger of Phariseeism. The spirit of self-sufficiency must be guarded against. Nebuchadnezzar was walking in the royal palace of Babylon and thus the king spake and said: "Is not this great Babylon, which I have built for the royal dwelling place, by the might of my power and for the glory of my majesty?" And the historian says that, "while the word was in the king's mouth, there fell a voice from heaven saying, 'The kingdom is departed from thee. Thou shalt be driven from men, and thy dwelling shall be with the beasts of the fields.'" And so it came to pass.[3] Beware of boasting of what we

---

[1] Zechariah 4:6
[2] 1 Corinthians 3:6
[3] Daniel 4:30-32

have done, are doing, and can do. A sense of human weakness and dependence on God ought to be cultivated. Paul said: "When I am weak then I am strong."[1]

Rationalism is a danger point. Much attention, and with great propriety, has been given to the logic of the discourses and epistles of the holy men to whom we are indebted for the New Testament. In our study of the Word, God has enabled us to arrange in a logical and simple manner the steps leading to an assurance of salvation. One may mistake following this arrangement for the faith by which passage is made out of the kingdom of Satan into that of God's dear Son. Such an error is so serious as to be fatal. The faith by which one is saved is a personal trust in the Son of God. It is possible to hold to an illogical arrangement of the steps leading up to a knowledge of salvation, with the possession of the liberty that belongs to a child of God; while there may be a clear understanding of the plan of salvation, without the freedom from sin graciously offered to man in Christ Jesus the Lord. Belief in Christ, not logic; faith in the Son of God, not philosophy; is the way of deliverance from sin. All is of God as he reveals himself in Christ. Guard this point.

Beware of shallow views of sin and salvation. No one can tell what sin is as God sees it. But God sees and knows sin as it is. Study sin, standing near the cross. Look into the face of the Son of God as he suffers for sin and then attempt to tell what sin is. Linger in the midst of the crucifixion scenes as they are placed before our minds in the New Testament in order to understand, as far as finite minds can understand, the nature of sin. Our redemption from sin is through the sacrifice of the Just One. Nothing that we can think, or say, or do, apart from the atoning death of the Son of God can bring freedom from sin. Deliverance from sin is through the favor of God. "By grace have ye been saved."[2] "According to his mercy he saved us"[3] The word "great" is

---

[1] 2 Corinthians 12:10
[2] Ephesians 2:8
[3] Titus 3:5

used to characterize this salvation.[1] How "great?" No man can answer. Our salvation is yet incomplete. We are in process of salvation. Read the following: "And the Lord added to them day by day those that were being saved."[2] "The word of the cross is to them that are perishing foolishness; but unto us which are being saved it is the power of God."[3] "We are a sweet savor of Christ unto God, in them that are being saved, and in them that are perishing."[4] "Now is our salvation nearer than when we believed."[5] "It is not yet made manifest what we shall be;" but "we shall be like him."[6] If we do not fully understand sin, no more do we comprehend salvation. Avoid shallow views of sin and salvation.

REVIEW.

1. What is the subject of this chapter?
2. Recite the language of Dr. Pierson.
3. Do these words suggest danger points to which the Disciples are exposed?
4. Mention some of our perils named in this chapter.
5. Do you think of other dangers?
6. What are they?
7. Against what are Disciples especially warned?

---

[1] Hebrews 2:3
[2] Acts 2:47
[3] 1 Corinthians 1:18
[4] 2 Corinthians 2:15
[5] Romans 13:11
[6] 1 John 3:2

Chapter Twenty-Two

THE WORLD'S INDEBTEDNESS TO THE DISCIPLES.

It must be evident to all who have carefully considered the facts contained in the preceding chapters that the Disciples of Christ came into existence without the determination of any man, or company of men. The movement described on the foregoing pages is clearly of God.

The world is indebted to the Disciples for:

1. *A more rational and satisfactory manner of studying the Bible than had previously been employed*. They were the first to call attention to a proper division of the Word. The Old Testament and the New Testament are the two great divisions of the Scripture. The Old Testament contains an account of the religion of the Patriarchs and Jews, and predictions concerning the Messiah. It is divided into the Law, the Prophets, and the Psalms.[1] The book of Genesis is, as its name signifies, "The Book of Beginnings." Exodus, as its name implies, contains an account of the release of the people of Israel from their bondage in Egypt. The Book of Leviticus gives an account of the tribe of Levi, the Levitical priesthood, and the ancient religious ritual of the Hebrew people. In Numbers we read of the census of the people who, under

---

[1] Luke 24:44

Moses, came out of bondage into liberty. Deuteronomy is a repetition of the laws by which the Hebrew Commonwealth and Church were to be governed. The book of Judges contains a history of the people after their settlement in Canaan, and before a king reigned over them. Men, and women, from time to time were raised up, called judges, to deliver the people from their oppressors. The book of Ruth is a literary gem in which is placed before the mind a beautiful picture of life among the people of Israel in the days of the judges. The books of Samuel, Kings, Chronicles, Nehemiah, Ezra, and Esther, are historic in their character. The Hebrew prophets were preachers of righteousness and seers, and ought to be read in connection with the history of the period to which they belong. The book of Psalms is the ancient Hebrew hymn book, etc.

The New Testament contains an account of the belief and conduct of the early Christians, and records the fulfillment of the Messianic prophecies. The four Gospels answer the question: "Who is Jesus?" The book of Acts contains an answer to the question: "How can the sinner come to an assurance of salvation?" It is the revival book of the Bible. From it we learn what the gospel is, as preached by men under the immediate inspiration of the Holy Spirit, and how sinners became Christians under their ministry. The examples of conversion given in this portion of the New Testament have the divine approval and are for our instruction. The Epistles show the application of gospel principles to daily life. The Revelation shows that out of the conflict between truth and error, light and darkness, righteousness and sin, God and Satan; truth, light, righteousness, and God, will be victorious.

The Old Testament is not complete without the New; the New Testament is not complete without the Old.

2. *The discovery, exposition, and practical application of the creed of Christianity*. What is this creed? Nathaniel said to Jesus: "Rabbi, thou art the Son of God; thou art the King of Israel."[1] Martha said: "I have

---

[1] John 1:49

believed that thou art the Christ, the Son of God, even he that comes into the world."[1] After the discourse in the Capernaum synagogue Simon Peter said: "We believe and know that thou art the Holy One of God."[2] In Caesarea Philippi he said: "Thou art the Christ, the Son of the Living God."[3] The verbal creed of Christianity is a proposition setting forth the nature and official dignity of Jesus. He is the Christ the Son of the Living God and, consequently, the author of eternal salvation to all who believe in and obey him.[4] It is belief in the Christ, not faith in doctrines, by which sinners are saved. Personal faith in a personal Savior saves.

Faith and opinion are not the same. Faith rests on express declarations of Scripture; an opinion is a conclusion, or inference, not necessarily involved in Scripture premises. Unity of faith, not unity of opinion, is required by New Testament teaching. There are, therefore, numerous exhortations to exercise mutual forbearance.[5] Paul was anxious to discriminate between his own opinions and a clear "thus saith the Lord."[6]

When one applies for baptism and membership in a congregation of Disciples no questions are asked about opinions such as: "Are you a Calvinist?" "Are you an Armenian?" "Are you a Universalist?" but, "Do you believe in your heart that Jesus is the Christ the Son of the living God?" The assumption is that if one thinks right and feels right about the Christ, He will guide him in the way of righteousness.

III. *The world is also indebted to the Disciples for their clear, constant, emphatic, testimony concerning the sin of schism; and for the earnest and Scriptural plea they make, and have made from the first, in favor of unity by a return, in faith and life, to New Testament Christianity*. They protested against the sin of division when others apolo-

---

[1] John 11:27
[2] John 6:69
[3] Matthew 16:16
[4] Acts 16:31; Hebrews 5:9
[5] Romans 14
[6] 1 Corinthians 7:25-26, 40; 11:1-16

gized for and excused it. The present wide-spread interest in the cause of unity and union among believers is a result, in large degree, of their Scriptural teaching on this subject. From the beginning of their history they have said, in effect: "Let us return to Christ as he is revealed to us in the Bible and strive to be and to do all that he desires us to be and do." Hence their formal proposition to Christendom is that believers shall come together and be one on, 1 The Primitive Creed; 2, The Primitive Ordinances; and 3, The Primitive Life.

IV. Their fundamental principle has led them to indicate **the steps to be taken in turning to God** as (1) Faith in Christ, (2) repentance toward God, (3) confession of Jesus as the Son of God and a personal Savior, (4) baptism in his name. The person who takes these steps can say: "I know that I am a Christian." Such confidence is begotten by the Word of God.

For the things here mentioned the world owes the Disciples of Christ a debt of gratitude.

REVIEW.
1. With whom did this movement for the reunion of the church originate, man or God?
2. For what is the world indebted to the Disciples of Christ?
3. Do you think of any other items?
4. What is their method of Bible study?
5. What do they say about the Old Testament?
6. What do they say about the New Testament?
7. What is the creed of Christianity?
8. What is the difference between faith and opinion?
9. What questions are asked of one who desires to become a member of the church?
10. What are the three items in the basis of union proposed by the Disciples?
11. Explain each of these items.

$\mathcal{A}$PPENDIX:

The Annals of the Disciples of Christ

1763	Thomas Campbell born in Ireland.
1772	Barton W. Stone born in Maryland.
1788	Alexander Campbell born in Ireland.
1792	James O'Kelly and followers secede from the Methodist Church and take the Bible as their only rule of faith.
1796	Walter Scott born in Scotland.
1800	Abner Jones, a Baptist minister, organized a church on the Bible alone. John Rogers born in Kentucky.
1801	The great revival at Cane Ridge conducted by B. W. Stone. Robert Marshall, John Dunlavy, Barton W. Stone, Richard McNemar, and John Thompson withdraw from the Lexington Synod.
1804	Cane Ridge Church, the oldest in the brotherhood, organized at Cane Ridge, Kentucky, taking the Bible as the only rule of faith and practice.
1807	Thomas Campbell emigrates to America
1808	A. Campbell and his father's family ship wrecked.
1809	A. Campbell severs his connection with the Seceder Church in Glasgow, Scotland. The famous declaration accepted—"Where the Scriptures speak, we speak; where the Scriptures are silent, we are

	silent." The Christian Association of Washington formed, composed of Brush Run and Cross Road churches.
1810	A. Campbell preaches his first sermon near Washington, PA. Church in New York Coty organized with the Bible as their only rule of faith.
1813	The Campbells and the Brush Run church unite with the Redstone Baptist Association.
1816	A. Campbell delivers his sermon on the Law before the Baptist Association.
1817	W.K. Pendleton born in Virginia.
1818	A. Campbell founds Buffalo Seminary. Walter Scott arrives in America.
1820	Isaac Errett born in New York. Campbell and Walked Debate on Baptism. The Mahoning Baptist Association organized.
1823	The *Christian Baptist* founded by Alexander Campbell. The Campbell/McCalla Debate
1824	The Wellsburg congregation unites with the Western Reserve Baptist Association. A. Campbell meets Barton W. Stone at Georgetown, Ky. P.S. Fall and the congregation in Lexington, Ky., accept the Bible as their only rule of faith and practice.
1826	A. Campbell publishes a new translation of the New Testament, based on the translation of George Campbell, McKnight, and Doddridge, known as "the Living Oracles." The church at Nashville, TN, under the labors of P.S. Fall, accept the Bible as their only rule of faith and practice. Barton W. Stone founds *The Christian Messenger*.
1827	The Mahoning Association sends out Walter Scott as an evangelist. Walter Scott baptizes a penitent believer on the confession of faith for the "remission of sins" at New Libson, Ohio.
1828	Boone Creek Baptist Association disbands to become an

	annual meeting. John Smith and many others in Kentucky reject the Calvinistic Confession of Faith and leave the Baptist Church.
1829	The Disciples greatly increase and multiply in Ohio, under the labors of Walter Scott, A. Bentley, W.S. Hayden, Marcus Bosworth, and others. The Campbell/Owen Debate in Cincinnati, Ohio.
1830	The Baptists withdraw from the "Reformers," and the latter become a distinct people. Alexander Campbell founds *The Millennial Harbinger*. Mahoning and Stillwater Associations become annual meetings. Campbell/Jennings Debate at Nashville.
1831	New Lisbon, Ohio, Cooperation organized. John T. Johnson leaves the Baptist Church. Union between "Christians" and "Reformers" in Kentucky.
1832	John Smith and John Rogers sent out as evangelists in Kentucky and supported by Cooperation. Reformers withdraw from Baptists in Richmond, VA.
1835	Alexander Campbell compiles *Christian Hymn Book*. Publishes "The Christian System."
1836	Bacon College founded at Georgetown, Ky.
1837	Campbell/Purcell Debate at Cincinnati, Ohio. First missionary meetings in Missouri and the West.
1838	Campbell/Skinner Debate
1840	Bethany College founded
1841	Bethany College opened with Alexander Campbell (president), four professors, and one hundred students. Benjamin Franklin founds *The Reformer* at Centerville, Ind.
1843	Campbell/Rice Debate at Lexington, Ky.
1845	Campbell, as Chairman of a Committee of Five, presents report for cooperation of churches in mission work. The American Christian Bible Society organized at Cincinnati.
1847	Alexander Campbell visits Great Britain and is imprisoned

	in Scotland.
1848	Walnut Grove Academy, afterwards Eureka College, founded.
1849	The American Christian Missionary Society organized.
1850	Butler University founded, Irvington, Indiana. South Kentucky College founded, Hopkinsville, Ky. Dr. Barclay sent to Jerusalem as missionary. Hiram Eclectic Institute founded. Benjamin Franklin and D.S. Burnett become associated in the publication of the two papers, *The Reformer*, and *The Christian Age*.
1852	Alexander Campbell advocates missionary conventions to send men to preach the gospel.
1853	Christian University founded at Canton, Mo.
1854	Death of Thomas Campbell Dr. Barclay recalled as missionary to Jerusalem.
1855	Alexander Campbell revises the book of Acts for the Bible Union.
1856	Eureka College founded. Benjamin Franklin founds The American Christian Review. Daughters' College, Harrodsburg, Ky., founded.
1857	Bethany College burnt and rebuilt. Bacon College becomes Kentucky University. Eminence College founded, Eminence, Ky.
1858	J.O. Beardsley sent as missionary to Jamaica.
1863	Oskaloosa College founded, Oskaloosa, Iowa.
1865	Kentucky University moved from Harrodsburg to Lexington. *The Christian Standard* founded by Isaac Errett. Bible College founded at Lexington, Ky.
1866	Alexander Campbell died. W.K. Pendleton is elected president of Bethany College.
1867	Hiram Eclectic Institute becomes Hiram College.
1869	Hamilton College, Lexington, Ky., founded. Louisville plan of mission work adopted.
1873	Add-Ran Christian University, Thorp Springs, Tx., founded.

1874	Christian Woman's Board of Mission organized
1875	Foreign Christian Missionary Society organized. Isaac Errett, president. Southern Christian Institute founded at Edwards, Miss.
1876	Christian Woman's Board of Missions begins work in Jamaica. H.S. Earl first missionary sent to England.
1877	Dr. Holck sent as missionary to Denmark
1879	G.N. Shishmanian sent as missionary to Turkey.
1881	Drake University, Des Moines, Iowa, founded. President James A. Garfield died. A. Norton and G.L. Wharton sent to India: first missionaries to heathen lands.
1882	The Christian and the Evangelist unite and become the Christian Evangelist. The Christian Woman's Board of Missions sends four young ladies to India. A. McLean elected Corresponding Secretary of the Foreign Christians Missionary Society.
1883	Milligan College founded. G.T. Smith and C.E. Garst first missionaries sent to Japan.
1887	E.T. Williams and F.E. Meigs sent as missionaries to China.
1888	Isaac Errett died
1890	Cotner University founder at Lincoln, Neb.
1892	Ann Arbor Bible Chair founded
1895	Divinity House founded in Chicago with H.L. Willett, Dean. J.W. McGarvey becomes president of the Bible College, Lexington, Ky. A. McLean makes missionary tour around the world. Benjamin L. Smith becomes Corresponding Secretary of the American Christian Missionary Society. J.A. Lord becomes editor of *The Christian Standard*.

Also available from Cobb Publishing:

Sketches of Our Pioneers:
A Brief Restoration Movement History

Alexander Campbell: A Collection
Volumes 1 and 2

The Disciples of Christ:
Tracing the Restoration Movement (1809-1904)

Toils and Struggles of the Olden Times:
The Autobiography of Elder Samuel Rogers

Abner Jones: A Collection

Pardee Butler: The Definitive Collection

The Oliphant-Smith Debate
On The Existence of God

The Wallace-Stauffer Debate
On the Lord's Supper and Infant Baptism

The Hansen-Webster Debate
On Eschatology

The Holy Spirit in the Book of Acts
by Bradley S. Cobb

The Life of the Apostle Paul
by Barbara Dowell

Our books are available through Amazon.com, BarnesandNoble.com, TheCobbSix.com, and other fine bookstores. Contact us for more information: admin@TheCobbSix.com, (405) 964-3082